THE MUSHROOM PICKERS

PICKERS

BY JAKI MCCARRICK

SERVING THEATRE

SINCE 1830

WWW.SAMUELFRENCH.CO.UK
WWW.SAMUELFRENCH.COM

FOR AMATEUR PRODUCTION ENQUIRIES

UNITED KINGDOM AND WORLD
EXCLUDING NORTH AMERICA
plays@SamuelFrench-London.co.uk
020 7255 4302/01
Each title is subject to availability from Samuel French,

depending upon country of performance.

Author's Note

The Mushroom Pickers is essentially a quest play that
begins with Laura's return to the Irish border
town she left years before, during the 'Troubles'.
She believes that the emotional and psychological
fractures within herself will somehow be healed by
this homecoming. But the place to which Laura has
returned is itself a site of fracture and, from the
most unlikely source (Frank McElroy), she learns that
whatever her issues they cannot be resolved at home.

I was twelve years of age when my family left London
for the Irish border town of Dundalk. Until 2005
there were British military checkpoints between
Dundalk – and Newry in the North. I grew up then
with a strong sense of a divide between two places,
which, perhaps, would have been muted in some
way had we lived further North, in Belfast (the eye
of the storm, as it were), or in Dublin (a mere
fifty miles from the border but which, during the
Troubles, seemed to be a world apart). Imaginatively,
the border has, therefore, always held a power for
me. Not just because it is a place between two
different states, sets of identities etc – and all the
dramatic potentiality that comes with that – but
because of its obvious metaphorical potential. Borders
are sites of liminality; they are where the fractures
are – political, economic, social, psychological. The
sense of waiting for something to happen is palpable
in such places, life has a heightened quality, is never
fully at ease with itself.

The Mushroom Pickers is my first play, and I knew when I set out to write it that I wanted it to be a portrait of life as-it-is-lived in an area rarely referred to in modern Irish theatre. It owes much to my love of Chekhov and his ability to 'illuminate characters and speak with their tongue'. It is, finally, both a political play and a snapshot of life in a particular place and time.

Jaki McCarrick,
September 2015

The Mushroom Pickers was first produced by Theatrepublik at the Southwark Playhouse, London on 2nd May 2006. The cast was as follows:

PHILIP McDONALD . . . . Michael Culkin
LAURA McDONALD . . . . Catherine Cusack
NANCY TONER . . . . Caroline John
TOM McELROY . . . . Sam Kenyon
FRANK McELROY . . . . John Kirk
OWEN O'GORMAN . . . . David Rolston
Director . . . . Svetlana Dimcovic
Designer . . . . Polly Laurence
Lighting Designer . . . . Benjamin Polya
Sound Designers . . . . Simon Perkin
Gareth Burcher

Prior to this the play had a staged reading on the main stage of the Old Vic Theatre, London, with the following cast:

PHILIP McDONALD . . . . Michael Culkin
LAURA McDONALD . . . . Aisling McLaughlin
NANCY TONER . . . . Fidelma Cullen
TOM McELROY . . . . Gary Egan
FRANK McELROY . . . . Dermot Byrne
OWEN O'GORMAN . . . . Shane Gately
Director . . . . Jaki McCarrick

The Mushroom Pickers was presented by Alloy Theater Company at the Gene Frankel Theatre, New York, on February 12th, 2009, with the following cast:

PHILIP McDONALD . . . . Timothy Roselle
LAURA McDONALD . . . . Maxine Linehan
NANCY TONER . . . . Karen de la Penha
TOM McELROY . . . . David Sedgwick
FRANK McELROY . . . . Jonathan Tindle
OWEN O'GORMAN . . . . Drew Sutherland
Director . . . . Hondo Weiss-Richmond

CHARACTERS

FRANK McELROY – late thirties/early forties, manager of McElroy
Mushroom Nurseries. A loner with a past.

TOM McELROY – late thirties, Frank's brother,
co-runs the business. An ex-priest.

PHILIP McDONALD – fifties, Laura's widowed father.
Works part-time as a mushroom picker.

LAURA McDONALD – early thirties, Philip's daughter,
a promising actor recently returned to Monaghan from London.

NANCY TONER – fifties, a mushroom picker;
once a noted ballroom dancer.

OWEN O' GORMAN – thirties/forties a mushroom picker – with
Republican sympathies and a love for Nancy.

A stroke (/) denotes the point of interruption in overlapping dialogue.

Words in square brackets are not to be spoken.

TIME AND PLACE

Around 2002 (a few years after the signing of the Good Friday
Agreement, 1998). The action takes place in rural County Monaghan,
Ireland.

NOTE

The lines from Patrick Kavanagh's 'Inniskeen Road: July Evening',
'Shancoduff' and 'The Long Garden' are reprinted from *Collected Poems*,
edited by Antoinette Quinn (Allen Lane, 2004), by kind permission of
the Trustees of the Estate of the late Katherine B. Kavanagh, through the
Jonathan Williams Literary Agency.

Scene One

A small cottage house in Ballybay, Co. Monaghan. A fireplace to one side. Over the mantelpiece hangs a framed photograph of a young woman, with 'Raglan Road, 1954' typed on the bottom. A bunch of wrapped blue carnations are on the table. **PHILIP** *is standing looking out of the window while eating his cereal. He lightly marks some dance steps. Enter* **LAURA** *with the post,* **PHILIP** *stops dancing.* **LAURA** *sees flowers on the table, looks for and finds a vase, blows the dust off it.*

PHILIP Your mother would have appreciated those flowers.

LAURA She would.

PHILIP That was a good match. But pioneers and *pissheads* don't go.

LAURA They don't. *(goes to get water for flowers)*

PHILIP All the money I've wasted on her. I wish I could have back all the money and all the time I've wasted on that woman.

LAURA You're obviously not compatible.

PHILIP You wouldn't know what frame of mind she'd be in. With your mother it was always like... so... but with her, well. People who drink will always find some excuse.

LAURA *(off)* It's not that she's bad...

PHILIP Certainly she is.

LAURA ...she's just not like Mum. *(brings flowers back in the vase)* Can we put the light off please?

PHILIP No. I won't be able to read the paper.

1

LAURA You're not reading.

PHILIP I will be after my Weetabix.

LAURA But the curtains are open. People can see in.

PHILIP What harm?

LAURA It's depressing. *(she puts off the light)* I hate a light on in the day.

PHILIP Women.

LAURA No, not women. Stupid. *(puts on the radio)*

PHILIP Anyway, who's passing that'd be looking in?

Beat.

LAURA Will she go in do you think? She's always nice to me no matter what.

PHILIP Expect so. I got no sleep so I'll give it a skip myself. Tell the brothers I'll make up time tomorrow.

LAURA But how will I get to Clones?

PHILIP Ah! I'll drive ya up, don't worry. The truck can take you home.

LAURA Da! They pack them like sardines into that truck. It's embarrassing. Please pick me up.

PHILIP Aye. OK. *(puts on the light and reads the paper)* There's sweets over there.

LAURA Nancy's sweets?

PHILIP Mine! Yours if you want them now.

LAURA We'll see. *(puts off the light)* A woman's touch does wonders around this place.

PHILIP It does surely.

LAURA Don't be a stubborn get.

PHILIP No. She's no class of a woman at all. A class 'A' long string of misery, that's what she is.

LAURA You'll make it up. You always do.

PHILIP I'll hardly get rested with driving you there and picking you up again.

LAURA Exactly. You may as well come in and do a day's work.

PHILIP Let the bitch miss me.

LAURA You know, I think your whole life can be determined by which way your love affairs swing you.

PHILIP Well, what else is there?

LAURA Money? Paying the bills? Keeping the house in order? Mum would've…

PHILIP She'd want me to be happy.

LAURA So do I.

PHILIP Certainly you do.

LAURA Maybe you should visit the grave. *(exits to kitchen)*

PHILIP Maybe. *(looks at the photo over the mantelpiece)* Why have ya 'Raglan Road' typed up onto this photo?

LAURA *(off)* Only told you a thousand times. I'm staking a claim kind of thing. Mummy always said Patrick Kavanagh wrote that poem about her. Met her in the bookies in Dublin. A wee girl down from Monaghan working away in Grafton Street. Isn't that the story? Kavanagh had a penny bet and handed her the poem on a bit of paper.

PHILIP Ah, that fella was a moron.

LAURA *(off)* Wished she'd kept the bit of paper. Be worth a fortune now. Kavanagh seems to be getting his dues at last. 'It was the garden of the golden apples, / And when the Carrick train went by we knew/ That we could never die till something happened, /like wishing for a fruit that never grew.' That was the other one we did at school.

PHILIP What's that you're muttering out there?

LAURA People here in Kavanagh country are just choked up with jealousy.

PHILIP Kavanagh country me arse.

LAURA *(comes in with two cups of tea. Gives one to* **PHILIP**. *She goes back out and comes in with a bucket of fire fuel: briquettes, coal, sticks, some rolled-up paper, and some firelighters. Goes about trying to build a fire)* Maybe you should try a bit of poetry with Nancy. Women like that.

PHILIP Yes, but that's the proper stuff.

Beat.

LAURA Did you like any of the plays I was in at all I wonder?

PHILIP Some. When I could understand the gist of it. But that's all behind you now.

LAURA Aye. All gone. *(continues with the fire)* Remind me – who did you say was the eldest of the brothers?

PHILIP Frank, of course.

LAURA That's what I… but I wasn't… *(she stops. The fire won't light)* All right. This is where I begin to wonder if I made the right decision to come home. Why didn't you ever get central heating?

PHILIP Rubbish! Going to be a blinder of a day. You won't need a fire.

LAURA It's hot water I need. So I can stand under that hose you call a shower.

PHILIP Right. Use the firelighters and put the briquettes round them. *(she follows this instruction)* That's it.

LAURA Mam used do this every morning. And in darkest winter, too. I could never get up for school unless I knew it was warm down here – and there'd she'd be.

PHILIP A class piece of work that woman. I should know by now that a man can only get such a woman once in his life. If he's lucky. She'd be far advanced now with that fire I can tell you. But for a thirst on her. For the wee bottle of orange.

Pause.

LAURA Come with me to the grave next time.

PHILIP Best place for my flowers anyway.

LAURA Nancy's not so bad.

PHILIP Ah! Give it here. *(takes over building the fire)*

LAURA What's wrong with you?

PHILIP The woman said I couldn't dance. Says to me last night: "you loused up pretty big-time in Galway, you stupid bastard."

LAURA Was she drinking?

PHILIP Locked. Women should keep away from drink. From pubs as well.

LAURA Maybe you're just not compatible. I don't want you to suffer.

PHILIP We were late once in Galway so we lost the championship. But she was at fault last night. Cocked it up goodo but she'd not admit it. On top of all that I still offered to get her fish and chips.

LAURA And?

PHILIP She said she'd call the cops on me so I says, go on ya drunken whoor.

LAURA For fuck's sake.

PHILIP And I was so vexed I drove into a ditch the other side of the border.

LAURA Da! Why didn't you… are you hurt?

PHILIP I'm grand. Fella from Belfast helped. Grand lad. Said he'd never seen a Lada the like of mine – as old as mine and still in mint condition. But a ten ton bloody weight to push out of a ditch in the dead of night, I tell ya that. Folks are cagey across the border about helping a man stuck on the side of the road at that hour, and then you'd be nervous about the type of fella that *would* stop. Grand lad though. Ah! Nancy has her troubles.

LAURA Haven't we all. *(lights up a cigarette)*

PHILIP Says her house is haunted. Haunted! That one doesn't know what a haunted house is. *(puts on the TV by pressing on/off switch. Now the TV and radio are on.* **LAURA** *turns off the radio)*

Where's the plunger?

LAURA It's called – a 'remote control'.

PHILIP Any post?

LAURA *(sorts through the post on the table)* Hollywood contract for me. Dues for the church.

PHILIP The cheek.

LAURA Bloody barefaced. And all the goings on they had.

PHILIP Had – and are having. A bottomless pit of it, it seems. Mrs Reenan still collects them, ya know. The dues. Holds her hand out every week for the little envelope. "Your dues", she says to me in that whining voice. And I say, every single time, "there's no Jews living here, Mrs Reenan" but she never gets it.

He grabs the little packet of envelopes and throws them into the fire.

LAURA Now. Quarter past eight. I'll get myself together then we'll head.

Beat.

Suppose I'm glad to be home all the same, Da. *(exits upstairs)*

PHILIP *puts the TV off. Touches and smells flowers. Practices some steps. Looks at the picture of the woman. Puts on the light. Stokes the fire. Sings:*

> ON RAGLAN ROAD ON AN AUTUMN DAY I MET
> HER FIRST AND KNEW THAT HER DARK HAIR
> WOULD WEAVE A SNARE THAT I MIGHT ONE DAY
> RUE; I SAW THE DANGER, YET I WALKED ALONG
> THE ENCHANTED WAY, AND I SAID, LET GRIEF BE
> A FALLEN LEAF AT THE DAWNING OF THE DAY.

Sung to the air of The Dawning of The Day.

PHILIP But for a thirst on her. For the wee bottle of orange.

Fade lights.

Scene Two

McElroy Mushroom Nurseries. The mushroom nurseries consist of poly-tunnels: long semi-circular structures covered on the outside in black plastic. Inside the tunnels mushrooms grow in abundance in aisles of waist-high containers. There are packaging materials to one side, humidity and temperature apparatus to another. The radio is on. (LAURA is wearing lace gloves; the others – standard-issue latex)

NANCY Laura, is that yourself?

LAURA *(whispering)* Of course. Who else would I be? And why are you whispering?

NANCY *(low-voiced)* I had an argument with your father last night. I don't want him to see me.

LAURA Save the whispers. He's not here. Not coming in today at all except maybe to pick me up. I told Tom it was his back.

NANCY Ah, you're very loyal to him. A lovely quality. He takes a row very badly does Philip. While I can just keep on cracking the whip.

LAURA You're a regular trooper, Nancy.

NANCY Just because he doesn't take a drop he thinks that everyone else who does is an alcoholic.

LAURA He means well.

NANCY Anytime I'm down I take a few whiskeys, like any normal person, and you'd swear I was putting heroin into my veins the way your father carries on. He's so…

LAURA Dramatic?

OWEN "Come back Nancy Toner – you're missed at the Kesh, come back Nancy Toner to me". *(sung to the tune of Percy French's* Come Back Paddy Reilly To Ballyjamesduff*)*

NANCY Give over, Owen! Well, I didn't want to use that particular word with you in the acting and all, but ya know what I mean, Laura.

LAURA Certainly. I know what you mean.

NANCY Has anyone recognised you from the telly yet?

LAURA No! And, don't worry, I'm glad. Wouldn't want to be asked for my autograph with my hands and face covered in this shit, would I? Having to explain that I'm just earning a few bob while I sort out my life?

OWEN Will you be joining us tonight Nancy twinkle toes, now himself is out of the picture?

LAURA No time wasted there, eh Nancy?

NANCY Sure I said nothing to him. *(to* OWEN*)* I don't know what you're talking about.

OWEN Aha, you know rightly so you do. The lovebirds were heard scrapping over something. I was told. In The Kesh.

NANCY Well, you're as safe as houses amongst this ignorant lot, Laura. If yer not on reality telly – likes of him down there will know shag all about ya. Ya know, it's worse you're getting, Owen O'Gorman. Bloody worser. *(to* LAURA*)* Bad as your father is, he has the decorum at least to keep the small talk *quiet.* That's a big ignorant get. Tell him nothing.

OWEN The Kesh is not the same without you, Nancy.

NANCY Do yourself a favour Owen and find yourself a bloody Mrs O' Gorman.

OWEN Time has stolen all possibility of that. Anyway, there is a Mrs O' Gorman. Me darling mother. Though a man has needs no mother can provide.

NANCY Aw, get away from me you vegetable. *(Enter* **TOM McELROY***)* No hope for ya. A riddling if ever there was one. A big, ignorant, charmless riddling…

TOM Oh, there's always hope, Nancy. There's always hope.

NANCY Tom. And how are you this lovely autumn day?

TOM Not a bother. Let's hope it keeps up for the harvest party next week, eh? *(***TOM** *goes over to the thermometer to check temperature; he adjusts it slightly)* Has our Frank been in already?

No response from the pickers.

(towards **NANCY***)* Always up and about before any other body has stirred, roaming around the place on his lonesome. Some people never change, eh Nancy?

NANCY A leopard doesn't change his spots, Tom.

TOM Owen, I hope you're not slowing the ladies down with your tall tales?

OWEN Well, I was about to say, Tom, we had a queer visitor to The Kesh last night.

TOM Is that right? How queer d'you mean?

OWEN A crippled chuckie*. Lost his leg in an operation on the other side in '72.

TOM The Kesh is full of Ra** heads, Owen. Keep yourself away, man.

OWEN Says he'd secretly buried the leg in Dundalk Cemetery and called into the Kesh for old times sake purely to commiserate the anniversary of the loss of his limb. He bought every man in the place a pint.

TOM A generous gesture.

---

* Slang word, sometimes used in Ireland to refer to members of the IRA. It derives from the Irish *Tiocfaidh*, meaning 'come', from the IRA slogan, *Tiocfaidh ar la*, meaning 'our day will come.'
** Ra from IRA.

OWEN A decent fella. But he said things would be rearing up again in no time.

NANCY Aye. They will if the likes of you takes drink from the likes of him.

TOM Now, if Philip is laid up, Laura, you can always get the van to pick you up by your way you know?

LAURA Thanks Tom.

TOM How's the quality this morning, Nancy?

NANCY The best batch yet. They're beautiful altogether.

TOM Thank you, Jesus.

NANCY Thank you, Jesus, it is rightly.

TOM It's good to have you working for us, Laura. Yourself – and Nancy there of course – undoubtedly bring a bit of class to the place.

LAURA Glad to be of service, Tom.

TOM *(noticing* **LAURA***'s lace gloves)* And aren't they just the sweetest wee gloves. *(exit* **TOM***)*

NANCY The darling of them two lads he is. *(she sorts the punnets into a crate and stacks the crate on top of others)* Takes care of his mother. A sober eloquent son a woman would gladly have dwell in her house. One that would never leave his mother in a torment, with nothing but black hills and bloody ghosts for company.

OWEN "Come back Nancy Toner to me."

Enter **FRANK McELROY**. *He checks the collected punnets and adjusts* **TOM***'s thermometer settings. Walks through the aisles, stops by* **LAURA***.*

FRANK I see you haven't the chaperone today.

LAURA I explained to…

FRANK Will you be working the rest of the week?

LAURA I hope so. Only, the 'chaperone' has the wheels.

FRANK Well, if you can't come in with him, the van goes by your way, you know?

LAURA Yes. I took it once. It was a bit… cramped.

FRANK You get used to it. So, what you say was wrong with Philip?

LAURA Pulled something. In his back. I did tell Tom. He'll be in tomorrow.

FRANK Good. That's what I like to hear. Got to keep this ship afloat, you know?

Beat.

LAURA Look Frank, my understanding was that this job is, well, casual, you know? Is that right?

FRANK 'Casual' needs its planning too. I don't want no pickers one day then a million and one the next. In case you hadn't noticed this is a business we're running here.

Beat.

LAURA OK. I'll do my best to help you with your planning.

FRANK If you wouldn't mind.

Beat.

Our gloves not good enough for you?

LAURA They make my hands sweat.

FRANK Well, so long as you keep them babies the way we like them here I don't give a fuck what you wear.

LAURA *(aside)* Gimp.

FRANK *(moving further down aisle)* Well, Owen. How are ya?

OWEN Grand thanks, Frankie.

FRANK What you up to tonight? Anything fancy?

OWEN Heading out for one or ten pints. You know I hate the drink.

FRANK Aye, I know.

OWEN Straight to *The Black Kesh*, Frank. Before I see the Ma.

FRANK Aye. You don't like eating on an empty stomach.

OWEN That's it.

FRANK Nancy.

NANCY Frank. *(exit FRANK)*

Beat.

What was he wanting with you?

LAURA Prince Charming? He wanted to pin me down to exact working hours. That's precisely why I came to work in these tunnels. I thought it would be more casual, breezy like. In one day, off the next. Someone like that takes the joy out of it. He lives and breathes these little white mushrooms. There has to be something in that. Small, round, white frigid little fucks. I bet he even has a mushroom for a John Thomas.

NANCY A John …? Oh, Jesus, no. Isn't that the strong silent type? In my experience they usually are very well equipped.

LAURA He's also the moody and psychotic type. I can tell a mile off. And *they* usually have big problems in that department.

NANCY Well, I wouldn't be surprised. I wouldn't be surprised at all.

LAURA I don't need it. The hassle.

NANCY You don't.

LAURA Tom's sweet – but him!

NANCY The runt of the two.

LAURA Or maybe something that rhymes with runt.

NANCY *laughs.*

Ah, Nancy. You know, my mother always said, never let the sun go down on a row. So it's a shame you and dad didn't make it up.

NANCY There you are. Can't be helped.

Silence (apart from the radio).

LAURA I need a cigarette.

Takes off her gloves. Slips outside the tunnel door and bolts it.

Da was right. It *is* a blinder of a day. *(lights up her cigarette)* Got to quit. Soon. Just need to let this place wash over me. Relax. Take it all in. Then I'll get back on my feet.

Enter FRANK McELROY *– exiting from another tunnel.*

FRANK Not allowed to be alone in Ireland.

LAURA What's that supposed to mean?

FRANK Privacy. Having a moment to yourself. It's a sorta crime here. Means you're up to something. Like, just there – you were away with the fairies.

LAURA I'm on my break.

FRANK Always remember my father mentioning Philip McDonald had a daughter went over to London, did well in the acting.

LAURA Right.

FRANK A mystery as to why you're back in this god-forsaken place.

LAURA You can take the girl from Monaghan…

FRANK Oh aye. The unluckiest county in Ireland.

LAURA I like it.

Beat.

How d'you mean 'unlucky'?

FRANK The lotto, for instance. The big jackpot. Never been won in Monaghan. I find that a pure embarrassment.

LAURA A matter of time, surely?

FRANK Highest suicide rate in Ireland.

LAURA In Monaghan?

FRANK Aye. We're like the Slavs. Melancholic.

LAURA Well, I'm not home for the excitement. In need of a little respite, actually.

FRANK Respite is it? *(pause)* This must be a bit of a change for you then.

LAURA Yes. Gives me time to think.

FRANK God, that'd be a luxury for me!

LAURA Something new for me, too. Spent most of my life on a certain focused road, you know? 'Tunnel vision.' And I haven't done a lot of... reflection. So, this wonderful cultivated mushroom farm of yours, and Tom's, may well be the making of me.

FRANK That's funny.

Pause.

Sorry, I was a bit smart with you inside. This trigger tongue of mine.

LAURA No problem. I should head back in.

FRANK Ah, you're in no rush.

LAURA All right. If you say so.

Pause.

So. Why – mushrooms?

FRANK   My father started the business. He saw a rising sophistication in the Irish food markets and went for it. Wasn't for any particular passion for them.

LAURA   I wish I could make decisions like that. Cold, brutal and profitable.

FRANK   You need a cold brutal personality.

LAURA   Cigarette?

FRANK   Don't mind if I do. *(takes the offered cigarette,* **LAURA** *lights it)*

LAURA   Where is he now, your da?

FRANK   Bermuda.

LAURA   But your ma is here?

FRANK   She doesn't like the heat.

LAURA   You couldn't get much hotter than this.

FRANK   Sure you can. But this is good enough heat for me.

LAURA   Me too. I'd forgotten that Monaghan with the weather is Eden itself.

FRANK   Or, as they say around here – you can't beat it with a stick.

   Beat.

LAURA   And you've a great view of the lake.

FRANK   'Laura.' Is that your real name, like? Or is it one of those – flashy acting names?

LAURA   *Flashy?* The one thing I am not is flashy. I was named after a Sinatra song. Laura – I think it was called. She's a dream figure. Kind of appropriate.

FRANK   Is it?

LAURA   Aye. I'm a big dreamer.

FRANK Well, there's nothing the matter with that. We all need dreams. *(beat)* Just how big are these dreams?

LAURA Monstrously big. Ah, they *were* monstrously big. Copping on to myself at last.

Pause.

So what does Frank McElroy dream about?

FRANK What do I dream about? Mushrooms.

LAURA There you go.

FRANK But mostly the wilder variety growing in that there stretch of forest.

LAURA ?

FRANK I learned how to identify the different types of wild mushrooms when I worked in Poland. I'm aiming to supply the top restaurants of Dublin, Belfast and the rest of Europe for premium money. That's one of my dreams.

LAURA I wish you luck. Never tasted a wild mushroom before. Someday maybe.

FRANK Once you develop a taste for them they're very addictive. In Finland people are taught all about gathering mushrooms at school. I'd like to do that too: teach people the wonders of the forest floor.

LAURA Can – anyone go there? I mean could I go? Have a wee gander?

FRANK That's our land – up to the foothills. Take a walk certainly. But if you're here early enough tomorrow morning – that's the best time – after the dew – I'll show you where they grow, and if you're hungry enough, sure maybe we can do breakfast.

LAURA How early?

FRANK Seven. It'll be just bright.

LAURA If I can get there I will.

FRANK It's not for everyone.

LAURA I'd like to learn about the fruits of the forest floor.

FRANK Well, actually a mushroom's more an animal than a fruit. I'll be there anyways. Keep it under your hat mind. Tom and I don't always see eye to eye, but that's brothers for you, eh?

LAURA I should get back. Tear myself away from the hills, the lake, the car-less roads…

FRANK Ah, you're just a recently returned Paddy suffering from sensory deprivation. You'll soon start taking the place completely for granted like the rest of us. And that's the way it should be.

Blackout.

Scene Three

*In the same mushroom tunnel, towards the end of the
same evening. The radio is on.*

OWEN Read in the papers they're thinking of re-opening
the old railway line.

NANCY Is it a Peace Process thing?

OWEN I don't know.

NANCY Good if it happens. But don't hold your breath.

LAURA Meant to have been a great service.

NANCY It was. The Great Northern Railway. Used to link
the border counties to Dublin and Belfast, over to the
sea at Greenore – and up to Bundoran.

OWEN It's the border caused it all to close in the first place.

LAURA How come?

OWEN Too many checkpoints. Cavan crosses the border
six times, Monaghan as many.

NANCY Pure vandalism, that's what it was. Whose bright
idea was that anyway – to rip up the permanent
way, leave one train goin' North, Dublin to Belfast?
Plunged Cavan, Monaghan and Leitrim right into the
dark ages. Oh I remember the Monaghan trains well.
Easy to travel out from here then, see how the rest of
the world was doin'.

LAURA Mentioned in Kavanagh's poetry. The train to
Carrick.

NANCY Aw Jeez, don't be talking to him about poetry.

OWEN I'm a noted poet sure. Be as good as Patrick Kavanagh was now, tell you that for nothing.

NANCY If it rhymed with *The Black Kesh* you'd be the king of poetry.

OWEN And you'd be Queen.

NANCY Certainly I would not.

Beat.

LAURA Da will be up for me soon.

NANCY That's nice for you.

Beat.

LAURA He said you had – well, 'troubles'.

NANCY Troubles! Don't be talking. Laura, my dog disappeared a couple of weeks ago. Just left and never came back. That's when it started. Sometimes, when I'd say a few prayers, it would stop. Then, the other night, as God is my witness, I saw her.

LAURA Who?

NANCY Twenty one years I am in that house and only now, when my sons are gone, does the bitch decide to show up.

LAURA *Who?*

NANCY The ghost! A young woman! Oh, Jesus and Mary, the thought of it gives me the shits.

LAURA There has to be some kind of proper explanation for that, Nancy.

NANCY *(she follows an instruction sheet to reset temperature and air pressure controls)* I know rightly, and I wish it would hurry up coming. I like it when your father stays. Doesn't seem so bad then.

LAURA Ask him to stay then.

NANCY I can't have him thinking I *need* him. Needy people are lost people, they have no... bite.

LAURA What if I stayed up in the house as well?

NANCY I'm not that bad.

OWEN Wire mesh.

NANCY Wire mesh what?

OWEN Black Kesh. Wire mesh. It's a rhyme. See? I'm a bucking genius!

NANCY Aye. You're great.

LAURA Look, I have a... a dawn appointment... so to speak... that's if I go... in the forest... with... so it would be far handier for me to stay with you actually.

NANCY What about your father?

LAURA If he wants to stay – which I'm sure he will – you could 'allow' him to stay – for my sake. And if he doesn't want to, well, no harm done. I'll keep you company anyway.

NANCY Philip mightn't exactly want to stay. I was a bit on the cool side last night. *(she smiles)* Two in the morning and he wanted to get me fish and chips. Stupid bastard. What's this about a dawn appointment?

LAURA I'm meeting Frank McElroy. In the morning.

NANCY Don't be ridiculous!

OWEN Bangladesh.

LAURA AND NANCY Shut up, Owen!

LAURA It's an educational field trip. That's all it is. But he's probably taken a shine to my fine, cultured ways all the same.

NANCY Change in tone from the 'moody and psychopathic bastard' you were calling him earlier.

LAURA I didn't quite. But maybe I like bastards, Nancy. The challenge. Getting them to squeeze out all that buried tenderness.

NANCY Take it from me darlin', there has to be something to squeeze out in the first place. The more you look for signs of light in that apology for a man, the blacker it will get, believe me. Dawn appointment! I'm surprised you'd be seen dead with a gurrier the like of himself.

LAURA He's teaching me something.

NANCY They don't call Frank McElroy, the 'Grim Reaper' for nothing. That's all I'll say and under oath I'd swear I didn't. *(she moves quickly away)*

LAURA You will have to explain that Nancy twinkle toes.

Enter **PHILIP**. **NANCY** *feigns complete absorption in her work.*

Nancy!

PHILIP *(to* **LAURA***)* Are you ready?

LAURA What's with the limp?

PHILIP A bad back affects the whole machine. You did say it was my back to the lads?

LAURA Don't worry, you still have a career in mushroom picking.

PHILIP I have to act the part. You know yourself.

OWEN McDonald, how are ya?

PHILIP Grand. Grand.

LAURA I said the sciatica was down your left leg. And as you're limping with your right, it doesn't look good, Da.

PHILIP Ah, fuck me. Just saw Frank and Tom there out at the car. And I'd swear to Jesus they noticed. Only came up for you. Would ya credit it. A daughter of mine that couldn't coin an alibi when it counted.

LAURA I'm kidding. I said, Philip has a bad back. Nothing about left legs or right legs.

PHILIP I hope you said I had a *very* bad back. And not just an ordinary kind of backache that you could still do a day's work with. *(low)* Were you talking to her?

LAURA What's with you?

PHILIP I'm nervous. She makes me nervous. She makes me nervous whenever I see her.

LAURA I asked her if we should stay the night to help with her 'troubles'.

PHILIP And I suppose she said no.

LAURA Go over and ask her yourself. I'll wait for you by the car. *(exit* **LAURA***)*

NANCY Getting your daughter to lie for you. You're some specimen of a man, McDonald.

PHILIP I did hurt my back, actually.

NANCY Right. Yeah. How?

PHILIP When I was driving home last night at three in the morning – with my flowers and my sweets – something – *or someone* – was in the road. It was pitch-black and I couldn't see, so I, I swerved straight into a ditch. Across the border I was as well. Must have got whiplash. Then a passing motorist helped me push the car out. That did me no good either, I can tell you.

NANCY What did you see out there?

Beat.

PHILIP A woman. A woman ghost.

NANCY You're only saying that because of what I told you I saw. You're trying to give me hope.

PHILIP Sure what kind of hope is that Nancy?

NANCY Hope that I'm not going off me head. It's called corroboration. Are you sure now Philip that's what you saw?

PHILIP I said Hail Marys till I was blue in the face.

Beat.

NANCY Do you and Laura want to stay the night with me? She's arranged to come in early anyway.

PHILIP Maybe we will. Maybe we won't.

NANCY Why don't you follow the rules when you're dancing?

PHILIP Rules are there to be broken. Will you cook?

NANCY I'll cook.

OWEN Good evening, Nancy. Philip.

PHILIP Take it easy, Owen. Off to the pub?

OWEN Aye. Off for a feed of drink. *(exits)*

PHILIP Feckin' eejit.

NANCY *(sweetly – to annoy* **PHILIP***)* Goodnight, Owen!

PHILIP If you cook one of your fine meals – I'll help with the spuds.

NANCY You and your half-raw potatoes.

PHILIP You're the boss tonight.

NANCY Aye. In my house every bloody night.

PHILIP *(teasingly)* And what if the bed starts shaking tonight, what will you do then?

NANCY Don't you go provoking me in front of Laura.

PHILIP Your prince will keep vigil in the palace, and if the trouble rears up again I will prove to you once and for all, it's only an oul badger rumbling under the floorboards.

NANCY And the ghostly woman you said you saw in the road?

PHILIP Ghost or badger, be sure of this, whatever the fu... whatever it is has my sweetheart troubled, its days in County Monaghan are well and truly numbered.

Enter **FRANK**. *He tests the thermometer readings within the racks and prepares evening settings. As* **NANCY** *and* **PHILIP** *are about to leave,* **TOM** *enters.*

TOM Be sure and take care of that back, Philip.

NANCY Don't worry, Tom. He'll be here tomorrow.

Exit **NANCY** *and* **PHILIP**.

Pause.

TOM You check House Five already? *(checks texture of compost)*

FRANK Aye. I've checked House Five already.

TOM Just making sure.

FRANK Of?

TOM That we keep on top of things. That we keep on top of business.

FRANK You wouldn't know keeping on top of business if it hit you in the eye.

TOM What would you have me do – follow *you* around the place – see how *you* do it? It's me you're talking ta, remember?

FRANK Have you something to say to me, Tom?

Beat.

TOM Aye. Will... will you be home for supper? You know she'll be asking after you, like she always does.

FRANK Go to hell. *He exits.*

TOM   *(shouts after* **FRANK***)* Show me the way why don't you!
And may God forgive your sins.

Fade lights.

Scene Four

*Nighttime at **NANCY***'s *house. Similar in style to the McDonalds' house. Over the mantelpiece hangs an enlarged colour photo of **NANCY** in a ballroom gown holding a trophy. **PHILIP** and **NANCY** are asleep in separate rooms, making a cacophony of snoring sounds. **LAURA** is sitting by an open window, smoking.*

LAURA Considering the circumstances I really shouldn't be smoking. *(quoting her father, using his tone of voice etc:)* "Women shouldn't drink, women shouldn't smoke". I think Da would have all us women on a pedestal if he could. I mean, what could he know of my life? Surely he must think there is something very strange with a daughter who was hell-bent on 'success' choosing instead to spend her days setting down – "layers of equal parts peat and chalk till soft enough for spawn to fruit". Poor thing hasn't a clue. She would have understood – but mothers – where are they when you need them? Well, my baby is to have a Monaghan childhood, and I'll go for walks and I'll be happy, and I'll forget that life where I had grand dreams, some talent and absolutely no skin.

*A scream is heard from **NANCY**'s room. **PHILIP** continues to snore.*

Jesus Christ, what the fuck am I doing here?

***NANCY** runs out of her room to the living room, sees **LAURA** by the window and screams.*

Nancy, it's me, Laura.

NANCY stops screaming and quickly goes for the whiskey bottle in a cupboard underneath the television.

NANCY Did you hear it?

LAURA I heard you screaming. I heard dad snoring.

NANCY Well, it seemed to me the whole house was shaking. First the bed rattling and then rising up off the floor, leaving me in a complete state of paralysis. And then pounding noises like a herd of elephants was after marching through the house. You must have heard that racket, Laura?

LAURA I was lost in my thoughts, Nancy, and I think, maybe – there was something, but I couldn't be certain.

NANCY *(drinking straight out of the bottle)* Girl, you are either completely deaf or I'm going off my feckin' head. And where is that bowsy calls himself my Prince – because that was no badger. Oh yes. Snoring away as per usual.

A scream is heard from **PHILIP**'s *room and there are loud thumping noises. The two women are at first frozen and then go towards* **PHILIP**'s *room, decide against it and exit out of the house.* **PHILIP** *emerges from the room – shaken. The two women return.*

PHILIP Oh I see! *(staggering)* The two of yez leaving me in there with… that's no badger this time, Nancy. You'll have to sell this house.

NANCY I will not.

PHILIP Well, there is nothing you can do / about…

NANCY What do you mean? There's priests and house-blessings, and, and… an exorcism will do it / for sure…

PHILIP An *exorcism*? No! It's not that bad, Chris' sake. *(grabs the whiskey bottle from* **NANCY** *sits down and drinks from it himself)* Jesus! That stuff'd take a clipe out of your brains! I saw her, Nancy. She's only a girl. A wee skit of a thing that was wronged.

LAURA Da!

NANCY Did she speak to you?

PHILIP Oh she did. She said her baby got took off her like they did to young girls in Ireland years ago – and – and she hung herself in the room I am in tonight. The room I *was* in tonight.

NANCY I knew it! It was the eyes! Woman had eyes hankering after something. Certainly, she never appeared all the time the boys were growing up; if anything, this was a special place for them. Though you do hear of good ghosts you know, guardians…

LAURA This is ridiculous.

NANCY So maybe – she was here all along. But if she's looking for another *child* to be guarding – well my time is well gone.

LAURA Oh fuck.

NANCY I know – it was awful to hear, Laura, wasn't it! We were just going till the noises stopped, Philip. We'd have called the Guards if it had kept up.

PHILIP Would you go away! Would have drove off to your sisters more like – taking my daughter with you by the looks of things.

LAURA Stop it you two! Look, I've something to say – and then I want us all to try and get some sleep.

PHILIP I'll not be going back in there, I tell yez that. Tell me what?

NANCY What is it, Laura?

LAURA Now, it has absolutely nothing whatever to do with… because, as you know well, Da, there's no such thing as ghosts. But nonetheless…

PHILIP Spit it out, spit it out.

LAURA I'm pregnant.

Slight pause.

PHILIP You're what?

LAURA Pregnant. Going to have a baby. In about seven months.

NANCY This is too much.

PHILIP Why didn't you tell me earlier?

LAURA I wasn't sure – about things.

PHILIP Oh my god.

LAURA There you are.

PHILIP Oh my god.

LAURA Please say something else.

NANCY I'm delighted for you, Laura.

PHILIP Delighted and excited.

LAURA You're pissed off.

PHILIP I'm surprised.

LAURA Not half as surprised as I was.

PHILIP It's that fella. In London. The one she was living with. I thought you were getting married. Why don't you get married?

LAURA I told you. That life is all gone.

NANCY Herself is obviously here for you then Laura.

LAURA Obviously.

PHILIP Why didn't you tell me earlier?

LAURA I've just said. I wasn't certain about things.

NANCY This is a hungry ghost. I can tell. She'll guard that child if you let her.

LAURA Let's just get some sleep shall we?

PHILIP The times have changed, Nancy.

NANCY For the better. Most men are not worth tuppence. A child is better off without a father not worth tuppence.

PHILIP What will people think?

NANCY Do you care?

PHILIP No. I do not.

NANCY Well then.

LAURA You're pissed off.

PHILIP I'm surprised.

LAURA I wouldn't be the first unmarried woman in the world to get pregnant.

PHILIP Aye, I know. But you're my daughter.

LAURA We'll talk tomorrow. Everything will be clearer tomorrow.

PHILIP Things are not what they used to be, not by a long shot. But, Daughter, I'll always be there for you, you know that.

LAURA Aye. I know. Look – whatever it was has the two of you rattled so this night – it all seems to have abated now. *(pause)* Night Nancy. Night Da. *(kisses **NANCY** and* **PHILIP** *goodnight and exits)*

NANCY Night-night Laura.

Pause.

PHILIP I used to tell her I'd rather she came home and told me she was pregnant than put one of those wee bullock rings through her nose. Well, I tell ya now, Nancy, I think I would have all the nose-rings and earrings and the Siouxsie and her bloody Banshee punk-rock records rather than to have this day. An awful night's business it is altogether.

NANCY You'll get used to it.

PHILIP Sleep, that's what I need. And I'll not sleep now in that room ya have me in. Can I…

NANCY No. You can't.

PHILIP Right then.

NANCY *(pats the sofa)* I'll get you some blankets. *(exits)*

PHILIP Right you are. An awful night's business it is bloody rightly.

Fade lights.

Scene Five

Next morning. The edge of a forest. To one side a hut on the land. Inside the hut: a small table, pots, pans, cutlery and a small stove. Bare bulb hanging from centre.

FRANK and LAURA enter the forest area, laughing. They are both carrying small wicker baskets.

LAURA Nancy says it's like a guardian. That her sons were always 'minded' in that house and that it's looking now for some new 'ward' to mind and…

FRANK Ah ya can't believe in that bollocks, excuse my Gaelic.

LAURA Well, there was – atmosphere.

FRANK And the smell of Nancy's drink I bet. *(FRANK stops)* Now. Here we are.

LAURA takes in the space.

LAURA It's – magical.

FRANK *(at his most animated)* Around a thousand varieties grow in this country you know. Though less than thirty or so are edible. Here – I have Chanterelles, Shaggy Ink Caps, the Boletus Edulis, the Giant puffball over there – delicious fried and served with garlic bread and rocket leaves, and Oysters here – and this *(bending down to pull from soil)* big brown fella, king of the woodland – the horse mushroom. Breakfast material certainly.

LAURA has moved further down the space, a particular mushroom catching her eye.

33

Don't touch that one.

LAURA Why not?

FRANK Bad choice.

LAURA Is it poisonous?

FRANK Deadly. Destroying Angel they call her.

LAURA Why "her"?

FRANK I like to think there's no magic if it's a he. You only ever hear of a femme fatale, which is what I like to think this baby is. Rarely do you hear of a homme fatale.

LAURA I know plenty.

FRANK I'd say you do.

LAURA The oddest things.

FRANK Odd – and wonderful.

LAURA Maybe they only like to grow where they know people won't be much.

FRANK It's the soil too. Unique to these parts.

LAURA And what's so special about it?

FRANK It's sufficiently damp. And it has Pearse's blood in it.

LAURA What's that mean?

FRANK I was being cryptic.

LAURA Some kind of pesticide or fertiliser?

FRANK Oh the best.

LAURA What's this one?

FRANK Oh – that's a morel. Edible.

LAURA What's it taste like?

FRANK Meaty. Pick a couple.

LAURA And that one?

FRANK Girolle. Tastes like a Brazil nut.

LAURA Well, one of those in the basket then. *(slight pause)* I've missed out a crucial piece of information from my story.

FRANK Oh? What's that?

LAURA I'm pregnant.

Beat.

FRANK Seems your life is changing by the minute.

LAURA In a complete state of flux.

FRANK It certainly puts a twist in the story about Nancy's ghost.

Beat.

So, where's the father?

LAURA Too busy to be bothering about little details like a baby, that's for sure.

FRANK A selfish world you come from, Laura.

LAURA Yes, it is selfish.

FRANK And you're still smoking?

LAURA I will quit. I will. It should be easy – considering I've quit so much already.

FRANK Indeed. I don't know if a person can give up a life like that, baby or no baby.

LAURA Why the hell not?

FRANK See my theory is – in life you have to be what you are. Or else you'll be – how do they put it – like a house divided against itself. People should go forth. Always. And avoid, at all costs, naval gazing.

LAURA Naval gazing? What do you mean by that?

FRANK Pointless introspection. Bringing your head uncomfortably close to your own arse.

LAURA Some people aren't equipped to go after what they want. Not thick-skinned enough.

FRANK It's all relative. I watched someone close to me die once. In the war-zone that is less than ten miles from where we're standing. Put all my dreary little inconsequential fears into perspective, I can tell you.

LAURA Well, I was in London a long... I didn't want to think...

FRANK That across those hills were a people who were consistently held in contempt by their neighbours? About the families wrecked from what they lost in that war? About all that waste; wasted lives, opportunities. There was tragedy. There is tragedy. But still, Laura – there's a people who, despite all that happened, kept going day after day and never gave up. They prevailed.

LAURA I know all about those people – and what they lost.

Pause.

FRANK Of course you do. I'm sorry. I forgot.

Pause.

LAURA I wanted to go to Hollywood.

FRANK Is that...?

LAURA That's the monstrous dream.

FRANK And why didn't you go for fucks sake?

LAURA I was afraid.

FRANK Afraid of what? It's only another shit town.

LAURA It's a new town. And – maybe – it was like, the final stage of my dream couldn't turn out bad or I'd have no more dream, sort of thing. Besides, everyone knows it's a place for vain, foolish chancers.

FRANK I don't think you're vain or foolish. But I would say – in life one is either a chancer – or a passenger.

LAURA And which are you, Frank?

FRANK I worked over in London years ago in a bar in Kilburn. An old boy who'd been working on the sites forty years said to me once, "drive – don't drift". Well – I understood.

Pause.

LAURA Where will we cook them?

FRANK In my den.

LAURA Excuse me?

FRANK That there wee hut.

LAURA I'm not going in that hut with you.

FRANK Why not?

LAURA Just.

FRANK Fine. You're welcome to take these home with you.

He moves to bring his collected mushrooms over to the hut.

Just be careful of the mink.

LAURA Mink?

FRANK Wild mink. Not native. Some daft neighbour of ours decided to farm them about five years ago. Well, naturally they're vicious creatures and they all escaped. And they've been breeding all over the county ever since. Makes the walk of an evening round here a bit… hazardous.

LAURA What about the walk of a morning?

FRANK Well then you can see them.

Pause.

LAURA Cooking facilities?

FRANK Of course.

LAURA Right. Breakfast it is.

FRANK and LAURA walk towards, then enter, the hut.

FRANK puts on the light.

FRANK We picked too much.

LAURA *(looking around the hut)* Interesting. Like a monk's cell.

FRANK Sit.

He begins to make breakfast.

LAURA Do you ever make mistakes?

FRANK With mushrooms – knowledge is power. Got to know your stuff.

LAURA Like everything else.

FRANK Now. That should be enough.

LAURA Good. I'm starved to death. *(pause)* Ever try the magic variety?

FRANK Aye. Did you?

LAURA Once. Boiled in cider. I hallucinated.

FRANK What was it like for you?

LAURA Had a head on me like Medusa. I remember looking in a mirror then moving away, but my reflection remained in the glass. Freaked me out completely.

FRANK That's the old Liberty Cap for you. For a real trip you'd want to try the Amanita Muscaria. It's what Alice uses in Wonderland to change her height.

LAURA You tried that?

FRANK No. Inebriation isn't my thing. I don't like...

LAURA To lose control?

FRANK Aye. Something like that. *(pause)* What did your da say when you told him?

LAURA He said I should be with the father. He wants us to get married.

FRANK Do you want it?

LAURA I don't believe in marriage.

FRANK I meant the child.

LAURA Oh. That. Yes. I guess I do.

FRANK Things will be different for you.

LAURA Aye. They will.

Beat.

FRANK Tell me about your world. Your 'acting' world.

LAURA For me it was a roller-coaster. Work, no work. Fall in love during *Romeo and Juliet*, split up during *Measure for Measure*. No permanence. I had a feeling of homelessness all the time.

FRANK And now?

LAURA I don't have that feeling now.

FRANK *(stops what he's doing)* Damn it. Can you hear that?

LAURA What?

FRANK Helicopters. The bastards do insist on dropping in on our side.

He briefly leaves the hut and stands outside, watches the approaching helicopter intently. The sound increases as the helicopter is overhead.

LAURA And I thought things were supposed to have changed around here. *(beat)* Look – it's away now.

'Map-reading errors.' Isn't that what they used to call their visits this side?

FRANK *continues to watch the retreating helicopter.*

Silence.

So, who else have you brought to your den?

FRANK All my other victims.

LAURA Nancy said…*(***FRANK** *goes back to the hut,* **LAURA** *follows)*

FRANK What did Nancy say?

LAURA She said, you, were a bit of a dark horse.

FRANK Nancy likes to talk.

LAURA I've noticed. *(pause)* You spend a lot of time down here?

FRANK Aye. When I get the chance. One or two eggs?

LAURA One.

Beat.

FRANK They'll be going to the dance tonight in Carrick – Philip and Nancy.

LAURA Yes. The Oasis.

FRANK I was thinking of going. Philip's been nagging at me to go for months. He asked me to join himself and Nancy, maybe yourself if you're going.

LAURA I don't know. That kind of dance is so…

FRANK Provincial?

LAURA Old. Old time waltz's. Old people. Just very, you know, 'Joe Dolan', and very old.

FRANK I prefer them myself. Old people.

LAURA You do? Why?

FRANK They're survivors. More comfortable in their skin. I'm not too old to go to the dance with am I? *(puts two plates of the cooked breakfast on table)*

LAURA No. But I'm pregnant.

FRANK Not so as you can't have some fun in your life.

LAURA I…

FRANK It's just a dance.

LAURA I'll think about it.

Beat.

FRANK What does London man do for a living?

LAURA He's a 'totally integrated living-space' design consultant.

FRANK Longhand for decorator?

LAURA Longhand for dick.

FRANK I see.

LAURA There you go.

FRANK You know – I've been to Hollywood.

LAURA Hollywood County Down or USA?

FRANK USA. It's nothing special. But the right place to be for your trade, I'd say.

LAURA For now this is the right place for me. Home in Kavanagh country. With the mushrooms.

FRANK And the mink.

LAURA "A road, a mile of kingdom, I am king of banks and stones and every blooming thing."

Fade lights.

Scene Six

Later that evening at the McDonalds' house. **PHILIP** *is in the living room polishing his dancing shoes.*

LAURA *(off)* What!

PHILIP I want to ask you something.

LAURA *(enters. All dressed up)* Why do you always insist on having conversations with me from another room?

PHILIP I want to ask if this tie goes with this shirt.

LAURA It's grand.

PHILIP What about the hanky?

LAURA Fine.

PHILIP You're looking well.

LAURA Oh, I don't know. I feel a bit over the top.

PHILIP You're grand.

LAURA Am I showing?

PHILIP No.

LAURA I'm very confused.

PHILIP What's bothering you child?

LAURA I don't know what I'm doing.

PHILIP A bit late for confused.

LAURA This is not my kind of night out.

PHILIP Come on out with your da. There may not be too many opportunities to do that. I'm not getting any younger you know.

LAURA All right.

PHILIP Get back with the father. It's obvious that's what you should do.

LAURA No.

PHILIP Things are tough here. Not a thing to take lightly. You should go back.

LAURA No.

PHILIP You'll sort it out. Give up that oul smoking.

LAURA Why did you have to tell Frank about the dance? He's probably going to want to hang out with us.

PHILIP It's a free country, Laura. Any bleedther can go to a dance if he likes.

LAURA I liked things the way they were.

PHILIP I know, but baby or no baby, it's not healthy to keep yourself cooped up. Frank is only trying to be friendly.

LAURA Well, I think he likes me too much.

PHILIP Ah, not at all. That man has no time for women, let alone one that's up the… well, let's just say, he is a particularly busy person.

LAURA A fine compliment to be paying me.

PHILIP The man is only trying to lighten his load. I've been asking him to dances at Carrick for months. Do you think one of these blue carnations would go well?

LAURA Fabulous.

PHILIP And Nancy's staying the night. Clean sheets. That's good. And none of that bloody business going on in this house. Just the calm happy spirit of your mother keeping the place safe. Nancy likes it here, you know.

LAURA Let me do that for you. *(she fixes the carnation on his lapel)*

PHILIP Are you sure I don't look like I'm off to a wedding? Don't want her getting ideas.

LAURA You're lovely.

PHILIP What makes you think Frank is after you?

LAURA I feel it.

PHILIP Well, you just have to make it plain. Hit him between the eyes with it: sorry bucko – not interested.

LAURA Isn't that the problem though. I think I am.

PHILIP Well, you can't be.

LAURA Why can't I be?

PHILIP Because he's not the man for you.

LAURA And how would you know the man for me?

PHILIP Surely it's the father of the child you have?

LAURA It most certainly isn't.

PHILIP There's fantasy and there's reality. Frank is too busy with other things.

LAURA Like being the Grim Reaper for instance?

Pause.

PHILIP Who told you that?

LAURA Nancy.

PHILIP Fucking Nancy. Always telling people to keep their mouths shut about her business – while she goes blabbering away about everyone else's.

LAURA Why is Frank called the Grim Reaper? You better tell me, Da, because I near enough asked him myself today and I definitely will tonight.

PHILIP It's no one's business.

LAURA Do you want me in a relationship with 'the Grim Reaper' or don't you?

PHILIP No!

LAURA Then tell me.

PHILIP *(puts on his Frank Sinatra tape)* Wait now till I practice a few steps.

> **LAURA** *watches him mark steps, disapprovingly. She puts the music off.*

LAURA Tell me, Da!

PHILIP He – Frank – is, was, the headman of, the boys in this area.

LAURA The boys? What 'boys'?

PHILIP Jesus, do you remember nothing about life around here? There's only one boys. IRA.

LAURA Fuck off.

PHILIP Frank McElroy was the Chief-in-command of Ra operations this side of the border. He's part of the Continuity crowd that broke away. OK? I told you. He is a busy man.

LAURA Does that mean…

PHILIP Bank robberies, Post Office raids, bootlegging vodka, knee-capping, bombs on the tracks, the lot. The work of one mind. 'Grim Reaper' is way too complimentary for the things that man has /

LAURA It's not possible. He's far too – decent. He's a kind man. He couldn't have done. He cares for things.

PHILIP *Have* done? He's still doing! And will continue to do. He cares about our country, more than most, so he goes a bit further than most.

LAURA You sound like you approve!

PHILIP Well I… if only for the sake of your mother. But the man has to be an evil bastard all the same. And I don't want you to be more than… friendly… with him. It pays to be a little friendly with a man like that. *(carries on practising his steps)*

LAURA How do you know all this? How could you work for him knowing it too?

PHILIP Listen, there's a lot someone will tell a woman in a bar to get into her knickers.

LAURA Nancy! Nancy and her fucking 'don't tell anyone else' stories.

PHILIP Ah, it's not just her! You live in one place, Laura, stay in one place – you *know* – and pretty soon no one has to tell you very much at all. You can just smell it.

LAURA I don't believe it. You've just rubbished a man's character.

PHILIP He's a monster! But someone's got to man the barricades, you understand? Nothing's changed.

LAURA How could you work for him?

PHILIP You work for him as well, what are you talking about? No such thing anyway as 'clean business'. You must know that by now. C'mon, use your loaf.

LAURA If he is what you say he is, Mummy would not want you to support him. In any way. We agreed.

PHILIP We agreed.

LAURA People came to see you.

PHILIP And I said no. That no one else should suffer. Now, you should go back. It's obvious that's what you should do. Or he should move here.

LAURA Who?

PHILIP The father.

LAURA Yep. He could come mushroom picking as well and we could all play knee-deep-in-shite-happy- families.

Pause.

PHILIP *(Soothingly)* Do you want tea?

LAURA I'll find it very hard to look him in the eye tonight.

PHILIP Just don't go mentioning anything about horses and then we're all home safe and dry.

LAURA Horses. Tell me what the fuck about horses. You slipped that in for a reason. What?

PHILIP Ah Christ!

Beat.

Do you remember a certain racehorse went missing in Ireland a good few years back? Shergar t'was called.

LAURA Yeah. Of course. It was big news.

PHILIP Well, all I'm saying is, there is one living person, known now to us both, knows right well what happened to Shergar. And that's because he buried him.

Blackout.

Interval.

Scene Seven

NANCY's house. **PHILIP** *has cooked the meal and is clearing plates etc into the kitchen.*

LAURA It's nice to see dad happy.

NANCY I do my best love, but he's an awful pain in the arse at the best of times. Did you hear that darlin'?

PHILIP *(shouting in from kitchen)* I did, you hairy bitch.

NANCY What did I tell you?

LAURA You love teasing each other. From what I remember, my mother wasn't one for that. I suppose a person can be very different depending on the person they're with. Well, what I mean to say is...

NANCY I bring out the devil in him. But the man's as mad as a coot without my teasin'! God love him, but I think that business with your mother shook him rightly. More than he even realises.

Enter **PHILIP**. *Takes remaining plates from the table out to kitchen.*

LAURA Thanks Dad.

NANCY I'm getting used to spuds cooked half raw. Don't know if I like it.

PHILIP Ah you do.

NANCY The first husband was a sweet-talking gambling man. That's why I love your father.

PHILIP Just when I was getting used to the slagging.

48

NANCY He doesn't bet, and with him havin' no taste for drink, I'm kept out of *The Black Kesh* and on the straight and narrow. Well, as much as a woman like me who's had a hard life with a sweet-talking drunk of an absconded husband – and children who won't come home – can be.

PHILIP Come on Nancy, we'll show Laura the steps that will win us the County Monaghan Championship. *(they get up to dance. A knock on the door)* In the name of...

NANCY That'll be the statue.

PHILIP Fuck me, woman, what statue?

NANCY Tom McElroy with the Fatima statue that'll cool the devil that is in this house.

Quickly clears an area near, or on, the TV. Tidies herself.

With her fine features and ruby-red lips it's no ordinary statue, Philip. I've to make a little altar with flowers.

PHILIP I thought me and Laura staying over for the week was enough for ya?

NANCY *(answers the door)* Come in, come in, Tom.

TOM *(enters with statue)* Philip. Laura.

PHILIP Mr. McE.

TOM And how are you all doing?

PHILIP Grand. This the – statue – is it?

TOM Oh aye. Isn't she a beauty?

PHILIP Gorgeous.

LAURA Did Nancy tell you, Tom, about her spooky visitor?

TOM She did indeed.

NANCY Tom knows all about such things. He was once in the seminary. Isn't that so?

TOM It is surely. Have you the place put by for her? *(***NANCY*** shows* **TOM** *where to place statue)*

LAURA Why did you leave, Tom?

TOM A long story, eh Nancy? But when all was said and done – I realised I could do more good in the world than hidden away from it. Easy thing to be holy in God's house. The world is a greater challenge.

NANCY Right. I'll be setting a few candles and vases of flowers around the feet, like you told me.

PHILIP And what exactly is the purpose of all this flipping hocus-pocus?

TOM The statue comes all the way from Fatima. She has great healing powers. Well documented. I'm very lucky to have her.

NANCY We're very lucky to have her, Philip.

TOM Sure, only the other day one of the lads from the farm next door to us came in to me, desperate about a missing cow. His best cow as well. We all kneeled at the statue, said the rosary together, and all of a sudden he looked out the window – and there she was.

PHILIP Who?

TOM The cow.

PHILIP Oh. Right.

Beat.

NANCY Well, just till the end of the week, Tom. Thank you so much.

TOM You're very welcome. *(Beat)* Will youze be coming to the harvesting party on Friday?

PHILIP Wouldn't miss it for the world. A bit of craic, anyhow.

TOM Good. Right then. Best be getting back to my Errol Flynn video. You can't beat the old black and whites.

NANCY Were always a one for the films, Tom. You should have been an actor.

TOM Maybe I'll surprise myself one day and head off to Hollywood, hey Laura?

LAURA Acting's a tough life.

TOM Sure what isn't! Now, have faith in her being there for you, Nancy, and I'm mighty sure the devil's bag of tricks'll be a pretty useless thing in this house. I'll be seeing you all. Goodnight then.

NANCY Goodnight and thanks a million, Tom. *(she sees* **TOM** *out)*

PHILIP Feckin' eejit.

LAURA Ah, don't say that, Dad! His faith just makes him seem... odd, that's all.

NANCY *re-enters, unseen by* **PHILIP**.

PHILIP I bet he sleeps with that fucking statue.

NANCY That'd be the type of thing only you'd say.

PHILIP All those ex-priests are gone in the head. They can't get it off with any real-life flesh and blood woman because who the hell can live up to a perfect image like that? Personally, I think he's a daisy picker.

NANCY Philip McDonald you're not to talk like that in my house.

PHILIP Right. But I still think there's something odd about a fella who carries a statue around with him like a pet dog. And everyone knows Errol Flynn was an amphibian.

LAURA Amphibian?

PHILIP Aye. One of those that swings both ways if you know what I mean. Like a... a double adaptor.

LAURA The word is 'bisexual' and you know it.

NANCY We've got a guest, Philip. Watch your tongue.

Pause. They focus on the statue.

LAURA I think she looks like mum.

PHILIP Not at all.

LAURA The way I remember her anyway. The eyes, the lips.

PHILIP Not the way I remember her. Your mother was full of – life. Animated. *She's* just…

NANCY Your mother was a saint Laura. And her feature in our Fatima statue is as good a reason as any to have some faith in it. Now, you'll pray with me tonight, Philip McDonald, whether you like it or not.

PHILIP *(brightens himself up)* I will. After a dance.

NANCY You're determined to make light of the whole situation aren't you? I'm not joking. You are a grand master of trivialising everything.

LAURA Please Nancy. I'd love to see you dance.

PHILIP *puts on some music – a scratched 78 of* The Tennessee Waltz. PHILIP *and* NANCY *do an old time waltz. This continues for a few minutes, when loud bangs are heard.* LAURA *rushes to stop music.*

PHILIP Mother of…

NANCY It can't be. Quick. To the statue. We'll hold hands and we'll pray. Big fuck-off prayers.

PHILIP *(shouts up into the air)* Would you ever shag off and don't be annoying us.

The sound dies away.

NANCY Gone.

PHILIP For now anyways.

LAURA Look, it has to be an animal. Obvious that's what it is. *(there is a loud knock on the door)*

NANCY Jesus, Mary and… oh me heart. *(she slumps on the sofa)*

PHILIP In the name of… Nancy. Darling. Don't fret love. *(he goes over to console* **NANCY***)*

LAURA It's only the door, Nancy. I'll get it. *(exits)*

NANCY What did I do to deserve this, Philip? I'm being punished for something, God knows.

PHILIP That might have been just an ordinary badger. We don't know. Not really.

Enter **LAURA** *with* **FRANK**.

NANCY Frank! We've just had another visit.

PHILIP Made an awful racket, Frank. Whole room shook from top to bottom.

FRANK Ya know, I think I saw something.

LAURA What did you see?

FRANK Someone – or something – run into the hills from the side of the house.

PHILIP Jesus, you're joking.

FRANK No. I'm sure I saw… course it might have been an animal. Or animals. A crowd of mink maybe.

LAURA Did you hear the noise?

FRANK No. I'm sorry. I didn't.

NANCY Your brother was just here, Frank.

FRANK I've been looking for him. *(sees the statue)* Left his calling card I see.

NANCY That he did. Oh!

PHILIP What is it?

NANCY Me heart. Me heart.

PHILIP Come on in to the room and lie down, pet.

FRANK Please. Take the day off tomorrow, Nancy.

NANCY Oh, I'll be fine tomorrow. Goodnight, Frank.

   PHILIP *and* **NANCY** *exit to her bedroom.*

FRANK Your father's been a great comfort to Nancy since Padraig left.

LAURA Did you really see something?

FRANK I did. But I didn't tell the whole truth.

LAURA That can become a habit. *(she keeps a clear distance)*

FRANK Before she and Philip – Nancy used see a man called Brendan Molloy. As soon as her husband fecked off, Molloy moved in for the kill.

LAURA I know, Da told me about him. He pestered her.

FRANK I think it was Brendan Molloy I saw running up by the side of the house.

LAURA In a weird kind of a way, I hope you're right. Human troubles can at least be handled. So long as they think the house is haunted, no one is getting any peace. Nancy won't leave the place and dad won't leave Nancy.

FRANK So where does that leave you?

LAURA I'm glad to be of some comfort.

FRANK And who comforts you?

LAURA Giving – is its own reward.

FRANK You weren't at *The Oasis* on Friday.

LAURA I had a headache. I didn't feel like dancing.

FRANK I missed you.

LAURA ?

FRANK Yeh. I felt, kind of stood up. If you didn't feel like coming, sure in your condition, that's no problem. I mean, I wasn't put out. I had a great laugh.

Beat.

LAURA Tell me about Pearse's blood.

FRANK What are you talking about?

LAURA I'm talking about the special soil in that mushroom forest of yours. Look, I don't care if what I'm about to say here is out of line, because if it's true you'll do what you will anyway, and if it's not there'll only be – some embarrassment to contend with.

FRANK Fire away.

LAURA I know who and what you are. Look – maybe you should not stand so close – maybe you should move over there by the door. Yes, that's it.

FRANK This much or this much?

LAURA That's fine.

FRANK This is a safe distance is it?

LAURA They call you the Grim Reaper because you kill people. And as if that wasn't enough, I think that if your precious mushroom field ever got dug up they'd find in it the bones of a racehorse that went by the name of Shergar. And I'm thinking that the man who buried him might well be the same one that hid him, and fed him, and then murdered him. That's what I'm thinking.

FRANK That's a lot of big stuff to be thinking.

LAURA I couldn't think it and not say it.

FRANK Oh many do.

LAURA And I'm trying to understand why you, and people like you, think it's all for the good. For us. For future generations of – bloody mushroom pickers – right? Wrong. Despite my history, I do not share your politics. And I didn't ask you to be friendly with me. I'm well able to go about my business – friendless. I didn't want people intruding. That's why I came home. But, if someone does want to be my friend then I don't want lies and I don't know if I want to befriend a, a…

FRANK A murderer.

LAURA Fuck it, yes. Pearse means all that Padraig Pearse crap about soldier blood purifying the land, right?

FRANK Christ, you're confused.

LAURA You scare me now.

FRANK You've done a remarkably good job of scaring yourself.

LAURA Why aren't you denying it?

FRANK Is that what you wanted me to do?

LAURA Yes. That is what I'd hoped you would do.

FRANK Why?

LAURA Because I don't want it to be true.

FRANK Not wanting a thing to be true is enough for some people.

LAURA Not for me.

FRANK I have nothing to explain, Laura. Nothing to deny and nothing to confirm.

LAURA You were hoping to be my friend no matter what I thought?

FRANK Maybe I was.

LAURA A secret between people can kill…

FRANK Not if they accept that there are secrets between them.

LAURA Is that what you want?

FRANK I don't want to be your friend. Or, what I mean is…

LAURA I understand.

FRANK No. You don't. But I won't keep you here with half of you frightened that I might chop you up into little pieces – and the other half eager to affirm your accusation.

Pause.

LAURA I'm sorry.

FRANK For what?

LAURA I didn't have to say – that stuff. I need to think about things.

FRANK You could always call the cops and have them check out the place. Only, they've been to see me three or four times already over the years and found nothing.

LAURA Oh.

Pause.

FRANK Rumour – is a terrible thing.

LAURA And of course we can't be friends now.

FRANK No.

LAURA Only a friend would confront a friend the way I just did.

FRANK Maybe. But it'll be different now.

LAURA Aye. I know.

Long silence.

FRANK I got my first order today.

LAURA What... kind of order?

FRANK The Chanterelles.

LAURA Oh. That's brilliant.

FRANK And the Oysters. Things will start to move now.

LAURA A restaurant?

FRANK Michelin class. In Belfast. They have a couple of places in Dublin too, so I'm happy about it.

LAURA Great. What do Tom and your mother think?

FRANK Haven't told them yet.

LAURA It'll be a shame to see the mushrooms go.

FRANK Not at all. There'll be twice as many tomorrow. They hold no grudge for being picked.

LAURA What if they didn't come back?

FRANK They have no choice.

LAURA Strange wee things.

FRANK How so?

LAURA They're a kind of decay aren't they?

FRANK Yep. Mushrooms come from the same family as rust – and Athlete's Foot. Though you wouldn't want to put either of those into a pasta sauce. A meaty morrel risotto, a crunchy girolle bake – now those are dishes to die for.

Beat.

LAURA Can I get you a drink?

FRANK No, thank you. Are you still scared of me?

LAURA Yes.

Pause.

FRANK We have a big harvesting do down in the fields. An old tradition. When we had the farm, after the hay was gathered we'd do the same. Will you come?

LAURA I'll do my best.

FRANK Pearce… by the way, was the name of Nancy's dog.

LAURA Oh.

FRANK Nancy's dog is buried in the Mushroom field.

LAURA How did it get there?

FRANK I found him dead. He must have eaten one of the toadstools and been poisoned. Maybe it was old age. I didn't want to upset Nancy; sure the dog belonged to Padraig her son, the one… who left. I thought the kindest thing was to bury him and have done with it.

LAURA I see. Well what about all the rest of it?

FRANK About me being the Grim Reaper of County Monaghan, you mean? Ah now.

Pause.

LAURA She's missed that dog. I should say something.

FRANK I think she has enough on her plate for the minute. Anyway, Tom is away already. I'm sorry for having startled you all.

LAURA No. It's been a difficult night.

FRANK I'll go. 'Night, Laura. *(exit Frank)*

LAURA Goodnight.

> **LAURA** *closes and bolts the door and enters the living room. Sound of* **PHILIP***'s door opening.*

PHILIP *(off)* Everything all right?

LAURA Grand. Everything's grand. *(***PHILIP***'s door closes.* **LAURA** *goes towards statue, looks around her and tentatively kneels down: She's not done this in a long time)*

Dearest – Mother,

Watch over Nancy's house; take care of my baby; keep us all from harm's way. And please, put paid to my foolish longings, to these strange nocturnal thoughts I have… of a lost dark horse… buried in a Monaghan grave. Amen.

Fade lights.

Scene Eight

Mushroom Nurseries. The radio is on. **LAURA** *in an upstage aisle.* **TOM** *and* **NANCY** *downstage.* **TOM** *is doing 'quality control' – i.e. checking the baskets already collected.*

NANCY Even if I wanted to sell the place, the word is well out now and who in their right mind would pay a penny for it?

TOM And no more after the noises?

NANCY Not a peep. Your statue that kept the peace, Tom.

TOM Glad to hear it!

Beat.

Was Frank around your place last night by any chance?

NANCY Wasn't he looking for you at the house?!

TOM Why?

NANCY Jaysus I don't know. I thought youze had arranged to meet or something. Honestly, no offence Tom, but last night my house was like Grand Central Station with the amount of comings and goings. I literally fell into the chair near enough with a seizure.

TOM Frank likes to know all that's going on about the place. That's just the kind he is.

NANCY To be honest with you, I think he has a hankering after Laura. I reckon that's the real reason he came round.

TOM Tell me more.

NANCY Well it's not normal.

TOM What's not normal?

NANCY They had breakfast in the forest. Together. In some wee hut with a stove, she said.

TOM That's mighty peculiar.

NANCY She said it was 'only to try the new mushrooms'.

TOM What new mushrooms?

NANCY Ah, them wild lads that grow in the woods.

TOM Go on.

NANCY Well, Laura says there's millions of them. All under a canopy of coolin' shade. Sure I hear they're all the rage in the posh restaurants in Dublin now.

TOM He has a den by the lake. A long time since I've been there. I wouldn't like to think what he keeps in it.

NANCY A leopard doesn't change his spots, Tom.

TOM Personally I prefer the mushrooms we produce right here.

NANCY A mushroom is a mushroom is a mushroom.

TOM I hate all that fancy lark. Sign of the times, Nancy. We're living in a decadent society and worse it's getting.

NANCY And getting worser.

OWEN Where'd you say we'll be next week, Tom?

TOM We're thinking House Five, Owen.

OWEN Would that be the one between four and six?

NANCY Oh, ya know rightly it is.

TOM *(to NANCY)* And speaking of 'the other', did you hear the news this morning?

NANCY No?

TOM A bomb on the tracks. Just down after Newry. Must have been laid in the middle of the night because the Belfast Express was evacuated this morning.

NANCY And was it [IRA]?

TOM It was surely.

NANCY Them fellas never change. Sure in the end they're only hurting their own people.

TOM My sentiments entirely. As well you know.

> **LAURA** *brings her full basket to* **TOM**.

LAURA There you go, Tom. All the same shapes and sizes.

TOM Last flush that's why. Last flush best flush. But not as good as the wilder variety I hear.

LAURA *(glares at* **NANCY***)* Well I have to say Frank's wild one's do have a bit of a 'nutty zing' to them.

NANCY Tom knew nothing about them, Laura.

LAURA Of course he didn't. Until you told him. Frank told me it was no secret. He was lining up the customers probably before he got round to telling you.

TOM Whatever Frank does has always been his own business. Isn't that right Nancy?

NANCY True.

LAURA Maybe he wanted it all to be a big surprise. Well, if he did, the cat's out of the bag now. Don't tell him I told you, whatever you do.

NANCY Or me!

TOM Ladies – it's no problem. Honestly, neither of your names will cross my lips if the subject happens to come up. *(exit)*

LAURA Nancy, I did tell you Frank didn't want the world told about that mushroom field.

NANCY Well, I'm afraid you told the wrong person if you wanted secrecy. I do forget when I'm not supposed to repeat something. It's an old habit of mine that won't go away. Sorry love.

OWEN Jesus. What's going on in this place at all these days, hmm? Everyone's whispering.

LAURA Forget it, Nancy.

NANCY *(speaks up)* But I do have some bad news that is safe to tell everyone I think.

LAURA Yeh? What's that?

NANCY There was a bomb – on the tracks, last night. On the Newry side.

OWEN Oh. That's a problem.

LAURA It didn't go off?

NANCY No. But it was big enough to have blown Newry into the middle of next week.

LAURA But why plant a bomb on the only good track from the South to the North? That hurts both sides, surely?

OWEN Exactly. Can't disrupt one without disrupting the other. Gets everyone's attention that way.

NANCY They just want to create economic damage.

LAURA Do they succeed?

NANCY They do of course. You were hidden away too long in London, Laura. They'd have you believe there we're all done and dusted up here. And what's changed, Owen?

OWEN Nothing.

NANCY Children still leaving these parts like it was a reflex action, damn it. And God knows, I could have done with an extra pair of hands around the place. My home with the boys in it was the safest, happiest home. *(sobbing)* Oh, why doesn't he call or write?

LAURA Who?

NANCY Padraig. My son. My son with a harelip that couldn't be having a decent life anywhere but with those that love him. I don't even know where he is!

LAURA I'm sure he'll contact you soon.

NANCY Do you think?

LAURA How could anyone forget you, Nancy?

NANCY All that fucker Frank's fault.

LAURA Seems he hasn't a lot of pals around here.

NANCY He's responsible for Padraig going off the way he did. He said Padraig had a big mouth, and he would have to get out fast if he wanted to live.

OWEN I'm away outside ladies. For a wee smoke. *(OWEN exits)*

LAURA Right y'ar.

Beat.

Now come on Nancy, that's loose talk and you know it.

NANCY And my Padraig wouldn't say boo to a goose. Belongs at home and no place else. And he hasn't a big mouth at all. Although the harelip does make it look big. And when Padraig went, the dog went, and the ghost came. My life is a bloody shambles.

LAURA Stop it. For whatever it's worth, you have Philip and you have me.

NANCY Lately, all I want is the bottle.

LAURA Keep to the praying, Nancy. It makes your face light up.

NANCY Oh, you're so lucky.

LAURA Why?

NANCY To be pregnant and young and starting over with no bollocks of a man hanging over you.

LAURA Lovely image that, Nancy. *(beat)* Besides, I don't always feel so lucky.

NANCY You should. You have it all before you. But let's get back to work, for work is the cure for all ills.

LAURA I've things to sort out.

NANCY You're well sorted.

LAURA I'm a square peg in a round hole.

NANCY Let us think of the harvest party on Friday. In the time of year they used call Lughnasa, and I'll be dancing a tango the like of which these Monaghan bastards have never seen.

LAURA You'll be magnificent.

NANCY Ah, I was magnificent. I had invitations to dance and teach all over the known world.

LAURA They'll come again.

NANCY No. The like of that opportunity doesn't come again. Before you know it there's a feckless husband and a sick child to absorb all a body's inclinations to fly. I never had a plan that was my problem, or a map to see where I might have gone, or what size my world was. But if I try hard, with your father remembering that the ballroom is not 'go as you please', there's rules, we might win the Monaghan Championship. And then this bloody place will be sorry it ever writ off Nancy Toner.

Fade lights.

Scene Nine

Harvest Festivities. A long table is set in a field. A barbecue. There is a ghetto blaster playing The Cult's She Sells Sanctuary. **OWEN** *is DJ (he has a penchant for eighties tunes).* **PHILIP** *is holding court.* **TOM** *is dancing – eighties style. Voices rise above the music.*

TOM Ah, Philip you make a great MC. The pickers are loving it. You have a great command with people as they say. Errol Flynn was exactly the same.

NANCY Don't think there's much of a comparison there now, Tom. It's Tarry Flynn you're thinking of.

PHILIP I should hope I'm nothing like either of them fecking eejit Flynns, excusing my language Mr. McE.

TOM I'll say a prayer for you, don't worry. *(PHILIP gestures to OWEN to turn the music down. OWEN does so – just a little)*

LAURA *(dishing out the food)* A great lover of Kavanagh aren't you dad.

TOM Sure isn't it a compliment I paid you when I compared you to Errol Flynn?

PHILIP Eh, no.

TOM If you say so.

OWEN Maybe you'll do me Ladies Choice later, eh Nancy?

PHILIP Don't fancy your chances of that, you.

OWEN Sure Nancy and me's been forming a deep and close bond, McDonald.

PHILIP Sunshine's getting to your head man. She's just toying with you.

NANCY Tom you love Hollywood. You must admit, it's what ruined your chances to be a priest. *(to* **LAURA***)* He'd be watching all the old films instead of reading the bible.

TOM Nancy you know rightly the two can be quite comfortable bedfellows and that's not why they kicked me out.

NANCY Aye. 'Family matters.'

TOM 'Family matters' exactly, Nancy.

PHILIP Ah Jaysus, we've got to get off that subject. Quick. Now! O'Gorman over there, you said you'd give us a rendition of Boolavogue. We'll have it now please. Wait now and I'll turn down this shite. *(goes to ghetto blaster and turns off music)*

Owen sings 'Boolavogue'

AT BOOLAVOGUE AS THE SUN WAS SETTING
O'ER THE BRIGHT MAY MEADOWS OF SHELMALIER
A REBEL HAND SET THE HEATHER BLAZING,
AND BROUGHT THE NEIGHBOURS FROM FAR AND
    NEAR. ETC

They all clap.

NANCY Ah that was beautiful, Owen. You have a beautiful voice. 'Angelic' is the word.

PHILIP *(finds a prime position, readies himself, as if for a recitation)* Now, when I was a lad, farming was real graft. None of this sunning yourself after picking a few mushrooms. I can remember my father setting off this time of year on a horse and cart filled with cabbages, travelling the guts of twenty mile to sell them at the market in Clones. Now that was backbreaking, heartbreaking *work.* Course it eventually killed him. That and the endless cutting and saving of turf and hay – but my point being – they – we – were made of different stuff in those days. Us *men*. Come spring, when the lambs 'd be slaughtered, there I'd be with my tin cup catching the warm blood as it fell from the lamb's throat *(some squeamishness from crowd;* **PHILIP** *is unruffled)* – then knocking it back goodo. Put hairs on a young fella's chest, I tell you. And we'd no such thing that time as your suicides and paedophiles, your bi this, your double that, your joy-riders, your...

OWEN Sure you'd no cars either, Philip.

Laughter at the interruption of **PHILIP**'s *story. Enter* **FRANK** *with basket of wild mushrooms.*

FRANK I see things are already in full swing.

PHILIP Mighty altogether, Frank.

FRANK *(to* **LAURA**) Glad you could make it.

LAURA So am I. It's a beautiful spread.

OWEN Weather held out for us, Frankie.

FRANK A grand day.

NANCY Terrible news about the bomb, Frank. You would think them fellas'd give it a rest once and for all, with the ceasefire and everything.

PHILIP British mythology, woman. There's never been a ceasefire.

FRANK This is the borderlands. The faultline. Ceasefire only means waiting. Nothing stops on a border without it flaring up again, eventually. As well we know.

OWEN Now that's what the crippled chuckie said in *The Black Kesh.*

FRANK There's a lot of talking done in *The Black Kesh*, Owen. Tom, I brought those mushrooms for you.

TOM Aw, I took a walk in that field of yours. Don't mind telling you, Frank, – I didn't like the look of them things at all. Misshapen, ugly looking creatures they are, god forgive me.

FRANK You have to taste them, brother. Try one of these oysters. There's plenty for everyone here, for the barbecue.

TOM I'll give it a skip if you don't mind.

FRANK Laura? I have something special here for you, too: another horse mushroom.

LAURA My favourite.

PHILIP Do you think is there money in it, Frank?

FRANK Rightly there is. Folks round here are always trying to farm things. They think money can only come from cows and sheep and Christmas turkeys, and land sold to Eircom for mobile phone pylons. But from one field of wild mushrooms, every penny I make is clear profit. I only owe god for the overheads. I will make Monaghan Europe's biggest exporter of field mushrooms. We have the perfect conditions. At last this godforsaken half-buried place reveals itself as perfection for at least one thing.

OWEN Chicken manure costs a fair bit of money. That'd eat into your profits all right.

FRANK No chicken manure or pasturisation needed.

PHILIP Ah, sure you're a great ideas man, Frank. Most of us could never think of something like that. It's money for nothing and the best of luck to you.

NANCY Does a man like yourself need more money, Frank?

FRANK There can never be enough money.

NANCY It solves nothing.

TOM Correct. Money only brings confusion and chaos.

FRANK What do you think, Laura?

LAURA Depends on what you need the money for.

FRANK Emergencies can happen anytime.

PHILIP I think it's time now for the oul foot display. What do you say, Nancy?

NANCY Ah, no!

OWEN Don't forget McDonald, I have Ladies' Choice.

PHILIP O'Gorman, I *am* the lady's choice.

LAURA Do, please Nancy. You were so good the other evening. Have you your music with you?

TOM Oh, I'll have to get the mother down to see this. *(exits)*

PHILIP *(pulls cassette out of his pocket)* I come prepared. The foxtrot. You see Nancy, I think of everything.

Music is put on and they dance. A slick act. **FRANK** *and* **LAURA** *sit on opposite benches. The dancing continues as they look on.* **FRANK** *asks* **LAURA** *to dance. Their dance is interrupted by* **TOM** *returning angrily to the scene and slamming the music off.*

FRANK What's up? Is Mam all right?

TOM No she bloody well isn't.

FRANK Well come out with it for fucks sake, what is it?

TOM The game's up Frank. She knows.

FRANK What in Christ's name are you talking about?

TOM The Guards are at the house and they want to talk to you about Sunday. You can't hide this and I won't cover for you! As god is my witness, it's gone on too bloody long.

FRANK Are they up there now?

TOM Course they are.

FRANK How is she?

TOM She's in bits you – you – you bloody wanker!

FRANK I better be going. *(exits)*

LAURA Is your mother all right, Tom?

TOM Well, she doesn't need any more bad news that's for sure. She wasn't up to the dancing anyways.

PHILIP What are youze all standing round for, gawping! Come on, Tom. You don't have to share your business with us, you know. We don't have to hear it.

*(**PHILIP** puts on his 'rebel songs' tape)*

LAURA Tom – what is it? What do they want with him?

TOM I can't say, damn it. But they're not here for the beer, put it like that. Frank's to be arrested this time that's for sure. And no amount of money will be able to bury this one. *(exit **LAURA**, hurriedly)*

***PHILIP** turns, ready to dance with **NANCY** – only to find **OWEN** and **NANCY** already dancing, cheek to cheek.*

Fade lights.

Scene Ten

By **FRANK**'s *den in the mushroom field.* **LAURA** *looks around, checking for mink. She peeps in the hut. Examines the mushrooms in the field, takes in the space. Sits on a tree-stump, takes a cigarette from her packet and ceremoniously lights up, draws on cigarette and enjoys it. Hears an approach; braces herself. Enter* **FRANK**.

FRANK I always find you.

LAURA Seems so.

FRANK Away with the fairies again?

LAURA I was trying to remember.

FRANK Remember?

LAURA Their names.

FRANK Girolle – like a Brazil nut. Morel – meaty, like chicken. Oyster – by the seat of beech. And Chestnut – with the coffee gills.

LAURA The way you say it. It's like music.

FRANK Laura. *(beat)* Thank you.

LAURA You're all right.

FRANK You didn't have to, you know. I didn't do it.

LAURA Not this time.

FRANK Though they still didn't believe you. Despite your acting ability, you obviously don't lie well.

LAURA I wouldn't want to see any friend of mine locked up. I don't think your mother would be up to that.

FRANK But you could have got yourself into very serious trouble. I didn't need you to lie and tell them I was with… they knew what group of people were involved, and it had nothing to do with – with my operations. They were playing games. They always do.

LAURA So you *are* the Grim Reaper then?

FRANK You're asking me that question? I couldn't even attempt to answer it. I'm a political man, yes. But if you want to judge me at least put the goddamn morality of the situation into a political context.

Pause.

Oh, why is this the way it is?

LAURA What do you mean?

FRANK Like this. *Our lives* are getting in the way.

LAURA Of what?

FRANK Possibilities.

LAURA What on earth do you mean by that? I'll never know you. Right now, I don't trust too easily. I require the full picture and you can't supply me with that.

FRANK You'll go back.

LAURA To London? No. Not now. I don't want to have my baby there or anywhere near it. At least I know what I don't want. I don't care if we're broke here. It's clean and healthy. Yes, it's bloody crazy, but there's space. You're wrong, I won't go back. Cigarette?

FRANK Aye. I will. Thank you. *(he smokes)*

LAURA That was my last.

FRANK Thanks. I feel really guilty now.

LAURA Don't. I quit. I wanted to enjoy it. Right here.

FRANK When the child is born – you'll die here without a focus. Someone like you has to have a mission. You can't quit your acting, you know it. If you didn't get pregnant believe me you'd still be in London with the man doing what you always did.

LAURA No. I would not.

FRANK And though you think you missed the lakes and hills here, you'd be glad you got away and became bigger than them and the people they hide.

LAURA But that's just it. I will never be bigger than this place. No matter what successes I had, here was, and is still, an enormous pull for me. It was my undoing long ago. But you are right, I can't kill my dream. I'll figure something out.

Slight pause.

FRANK Go to America.

LAURA Right.

FRANK Go to Hollywood. No, I'm serious. When the baby's born take a chance. Find out. It may be a disaster – but at least you'll have tried and you'll know.

LAURA How can I go? It costs money. A lot. And I wouldn't hit the fucking USA with a baby. Get real.

FRANK I know people there. People who owe me. Things could be sorted out. It would be my way of paying you back for helping me – even though you didn't really.

LAURA I couldn't accept that.

FRANK Couldn't or won't?

LAURA Both. But thanks anyway.

FRANK I don't understand. Why not?

LAURA Because I won't go. Because I'm fed up traipsing around the world with half a heart.

FRANK Because it's here, right?

LAURA Lost somewhere.

FRANK That's what I mean by naval gazing.

LAURA I know.

FRANK So you stay and play housewife.

LAURA NO.

FRANK Monaghan won't go away.

LAURA Jesus Christ. What's the difference between London and America? They're both the same. I could have got a break anywhere if I'd had all my pieces. My attachment to this place would get in the way anywhere. An actor needs to be in the city – and I have grown to hate the city.

FRANK Grow up. Who's talking about home? Think of it as business. Make your contacts, get the work and when you get it…

LAURA Do what? Stay there? Let five years pass? Same ole same ole.

FRANK If things go well you would have the freedom financially to come and go from here as much as you'd like without ever feeling stuck.

LAURA And if I failed?

FRANK You won't fail.

LAURA Kavanagh was the same as me. He had big dreams, went to Dublin and London. But the pull to here was huge. It's a disability. Over connected to the land and to its roundness – so that the lines, the tall straight buildings of the city – cause pain. I'm the same as that.

FRANK Then you are doomed. Claimed. By a land that will surely stunt you – and shut you out. You'll end up hating it.

LAURA You don't. Why should I?

FRANK What do you mean? I thrive on the hatred! I just take it across the border where it can be used!

Long pause.

LAURA She never even drank.

FRANK Who?

LAURA My mother. She only went into the bar for an orange juice after the bingo. Some say they heard the blast as far as Carrick. All I wanted to do was leave here after that. But I never once thought of revenge.

FRANK Isn't success the best revenge? Paddy Kavanagh might have missed us all but he knew what side his bread was buttered on.

LAURA I have to sort things out. I have doubts.

FRANK About?

LAURA The baby.

FRANK Take control.

LAURA Yes. *(pause)* Nancy's place was very cold last night. But the commotion seems to have stopped. Jeez, maybe it was the statue. I can still feel something there, though... something amiss.

FRANK Sure isn't there something amiss in every house? *(beat)* See, this is better.

LAURA What do you mean?

FRANK Between us. It's more – honest. *(beat)* You know, if you really listen one day, Laura, you might be able to hear... that.

LAURA What?

FRANK Ulster's heartbeat.

LAURA Isn't Ulster's heartbeat, my heartbeat, this child's heartbeat, and yours? I can hear that right enough.

FRANK No. In this land, awake or asleep, Ulster's heartbeat is the sound of the helicopter.

LAURA *(listening)* But none are up there now. It's all changed, Frank. It's called the Peace Process. We can not hear that sound from where we stand.

FRANK I can. I am compelled by that sound.

LAURA They told me the bomb was cabelled directly to the railway line. That it was linked to the army barracks on the border. What lay on the tracks at Newry was a decoy –

FRANK I know.

LAURA People might have died. Were they supposed to die?

FRANK Probably.

LAURA Do flesh and blood, human heartbeats mean nothing to you?

FRANK I can no longer hear that sound.

LAURA Then you too are doomed.

FRANK Maybe I'll hear it when the helicopters leave this land. For good. There'll be space then.

Beat.

LAURA You know what we're both guilty of?

FRANK Yeh?

LAURA Postponement.

FRANK Of what?

LAURA Living. *(pause)* Is that, that horse, Shergar, is he buried here – in the mushroom field?

FRANK On your first visit home from Hollywood I promise I'll tell you.

LAURA Jesus – why would you have me go – really?

FRANK I'd like to help a big dream.

LAURA So you'd be like a patron?

FRANK A nicer way of putting it. Better than Grim Reaper.

LAURA *(stands to go)* In London I'd battle with the memory of these bumpy hills and the mist of an autumn evening that hangs over every Monaghan lake – because I'd think to myself that it was all so sentimental, that I'd best be forgetting it, and carve into my brain once and for all that I was better off where I was. Where I had to be. To work. To serve culture. That I should let all this go. It was a battle I couldn't win. As soon as I saw them again I wanted to nestle into those hills like a baby. I don't miss what I left, but I've not found whatever I came home for either. *(pause)* The last flush of the mushrooms today, yes?

FRANK Yep. No more from that soil.

LAURA Then I should get back to work.

FRANK Did you eat?

LAURA This is an invite to the den, right?

FRANK I'm preparing for a new order. Same restaurant. I want to try a new combination.

LAURA Don't you ever get sick of them?

FRANK My '*grande passione*'?

LAURA *(in a teasing French accent)* Girolle, Morel *(then normal accent)* Shaggy inkcap. Bloody toadstool city if you ask me.

FRANK C'mon.

They go to pick mushrooms.

Fade lights.

Scene Eleven

A week later. In the Mushroom Tunnels. **PHILIP**,
OWEN, **NANCY** *and* **TOM** *are picking mushrooms in the
aisles.* **TOM** *at a separate end to the others; he attends to
temperature controls and takes notes etc. The radio is on.*

NANCY This is a good batch.

PHILIP Aye.

NANCY All the same sizes this time.

PHILIP Aye. The Tesco shoppers will be happy about it.

OWEN We'll be in next door from next week. (**OWEN**
changes the radio station)

Pause.

TOM Looking forward to the championship, Nancy?

NANCY We are.

OWEN Good luck to you.

NANCY Thanks.

A long period of silence.

Philip.

PHILIP Aagh! What?

NANCY Some of your things are still in the room.

PHILIP What things?

NANCY Few ties and a hanky.

PHILIP I'm in no hurry for them.

NANCY Just letting you know.

PHILIP Thanks love.

OWEN Guess what folks, heard someone from 'Blayney won the lottery.

NANCY Where was the ticket bought?

OWEN Dublin.

NANCY There you are.

OWEN There you go.

NANCY Are you going up tonight?

PHILIP To the hospital? I am.

NANCY I'll go with you. I'd like to go. She wouldn't be put out by that now, would she?

PHILIP No. She's a great wee girl.

NANCY A great wee girl. She's been through it, I'll say that for her. Very brave she's been altogether.

PHILIP Aye. She's taken it well.

NANCY It would be hard for any woman to lose a child, let alone one not yet born.

PHILIP Well, I suppose she's alive herself.

NANCY That was a miracle all on its own.

Pause.

PHILIP I could kill him. I'd like ta. I'd like ta kick the shite out of him.

NANCY You said what you had to say, Philip. And you were brave to do it at all considering the kind he is.

PHILIP I wasn't brave enough. He should have known better.

TOM (*shouts up from the other end of the tunnel*) Glad to see the lovebirds talking.

PHILIP When it comes down to it, the likes of them are all the same. Business comes first.

NANCY Tom is only trying to be nice. I'm sure he feels deeply for you, Philip.

PHILIP If I'd lost her as well I don't know what I'd do.

NANCY Well, you didn't. She's all right. She'll be fine.

PHILIP He should have known. He's supposed to be an expert isn't he? How could he not know he was picking the wrong kind of mushroom. *(chucks his box of collected mushrooms)* I can't bear to touch the cunts. How is it, of all the places he's been sending them out, it's my Laura that lies languishing in a hospital bed? He's not even sick, 'cept in his head,

NANCY He did tell you she picked some of them herself. He only made a mistake, Philip, a terrible mistake.

Another period of silence. **TOM** *moves closer to* **NANCY** *and* **PHILIP**.

TOM How is she doing?

PHILIP She's better now.

TOM I'm sorry about the…

PHILIP I'll tell her you said so, Mr. McE.

NANCY How's Frank?

TOM He can't understand how it happened at all. You see, he's precise in all he does our Frank. Never slips up. Walking around in a daze now so he is.

PHILIP I'll burn his fucking field for him.

TOM We should be glad Laura is spared. It was the most deadly in the field – "destroying angels" what did it. If you ever saw one – they are so obviously not for eating. I don't know how the hell it happened. One bad one just got in.

PHILIP He should have known.

TOM He should have known.

PHILIP I've already buried a wife and now I've lost my only grandchild. And I very nearly lost my daughter. I told her to keep away from him. Evil follows your brother, Tom.

TOM He just shouldn't have bothered with those mushrooms.

NANCY He was never happy with things as they are.

TOM The cultivated mushroom is the only safe one to eat. That's why they've been cultivated in the first place. Things are kept at the right temperature, and the right humidity, and we never make mistakes. It might be boring but this little thing never did anyone a bit of harm.

PHILIP It's a dirty business all the same.

TOM Sure what isn't? Everyone has to do something. I didn't even know Laura was pregnant before all of this.

PHILIP She didn't tell too many.

TOM *(low-voiced)* Was, a, our Frank… was he, well, you know…

PHILIP Jesus Christ, no. She wanted nothing to do with the father. It's as well now.

NANCY Oh, she's a grand wee girl. Only home from London and all the carry-on.

PHILIP All she wanted was a wee rest.

TOM Well, I have herself with me today. Fatima. We could pray. Pray as we pick sort of thing? *(slight pause)* OK, no. But she certainly licked the problems in your house, Nancy. Brought some peace to the place.

NANCY Oh, she did indeed. Thank you, Tom.

TOM You're welcome.

PHILIP Do you think so?

NANCY Well of course, Philip, you saw yourself. There hasn't been so much as a creaking floorboard in the last couple of days.

PHILIP I know. But 'peace'? Sure there's nothing of the sort! For what kind of peace – is a dead child, Nancy? This is what I get for it, ya know. Working for them. This is the price. Oh, it's not hard to see the man he is. So I should have known. *I* should have known.

Fade lights.

Scene Twelve

A few weeks later. In the wild mushroom field. The mushrooms are all gone. **FRANK** *is spreading compost over the fields. A helicopter can be heard in the distance. The sound is quite loud on stage and then fades away. Enter* **LAURA**. *He carries on working.*

FRANK Did you hear it?

Pause.

LAURA I hear the water lapping the rocks in the lake, and you scraping the earth there. But if you're asking me did I hear a helicopter, then no, I didn't. *(beat)* So. They really are all gone.

FRANK Packed up and left.

LAURA I thought you said they had a permanent home here in the wet shade?

FRANK They *had*. I've given them a bit of a sending off. Getting too wet now anyways. Next year perhaps.

Pause.

LAURA Da got another job. In a shop.

FRANK Selling... ?

LAURA Groceries. Sweets. Blue carnations. Value Stores in Ballybay. They know him there.

FRANK A good man, Philip. A good worker.

LAURA Too old for picking.

FRANK Has a heart of gold.

LAURA Thank you for the flowers.

FRANK He'll be missed.

LAURA We put them on my mother's grave.

FRANK I'm sorry about…

LAURA Yeah.

Beat.

FRANK I'm glad you're leaving now.

LAURA Why?

FRANK Your letters will remind me there is an interesting life possible for people.

LAURA You could have any life you wanted. That's what you said. Drive don't drift.

FRANK I could, but I am bound here..Needed.

LAURA So you say.

Beat.

He's still very angry with you.

FRANK Are you?

LAURA No.

FRANK You picked her yourself didn't you?

LAURA The one – no – not that I know of! It just – happened. I don't know how. Did you really think I did it myself? Poison myself? Kill my baby?

FRANK I thought about it.

LAURA Maybe you can't admit that you made a mistake. That you made a bad choice.

FRANK Then maybe I did.

LAURA Or maybe I did. It's too late now anyway. My child is dead.

FRANK I didn't mean to Laura…

LAURA What's done is done.

FRANK I probably got distracted…

LAURA Leave it, Frank.

FRANK … and didn't look and they all got cooked in the meal together.

LAURA Which *you* didn't eat.

FRANK Don't say that. Do you think there's been a day since it happened when I didn't wish I'd eaten every fucking scrap? I wished myself blind! I didn't want my world to touch you, Laura. I feel – cursed.

LAURA I know you didn't mean for what happened.

FRANK For a while you were in danger too.

LAURA Maybe my dreams were more resilient than I thought.

FRANK I'm glad I could do something.

LAURA Yes. My American business trip.

FRANK The very least I could do.

LAURA Here – is no longer a place of respite for me, Frank.

FRANK No.

LAURA But the peace has kept up in Nancy's house.

FRANK Aye. A word in Brendan Molloy's ear seems to have done the trick.

LAURA Was it really him all along?

FRANK He denied it of course. But the episode is over, and if people want to think there was something mystical to it like the power of faith in an old clay statue then let them think it. I've never had any luck with that. It's utterly ridiculous. I lambast them fellas with their bowler hats and orange sashes – while at home my own brother snuggles up at night to a Fatima statue. Thankfully, I've always been a realist.

LAURA They want to get married, dad and Nancy.

FRANK They should.

Pause.

I will be very alone when you go. More than before.

LAURA Then you will know how I feel to have lost my child. Maybe you need to know that feeling.

Pause.

The ceasefire is holding, Frank. They say the violence won't erupt again unless there's significant – fringe activity – in which case – you will probably be 'needed', as you put it.

FRANK To *reap* the harvest?

LAURA One day you might *be* the harvest.

FRANK So might all of us who take chances.

Beat.

LAURA I shall miss the place.

FRANK There is always something to miss. Don't let it hold you back. I mean it. I want to see headlines in the Northern Standard in six months time – 'Mushroom Picker makes good in Hollywood'.

LAURA We'll see. *(beat)* Mushroom picking isn't on my CV.

FRANK There's very little else on mine.

Beat.

LAURA What's that you were laying down?

FRANK The old compost from the tunnels. There's some goodness in it yet.

LAURA Don't blame yourself.

FRANK I have a bit of Kavanagh for you: "My black hills have never seen the sun rising – eternally they look north towards Armagh." Monaghan for some of us is not an easy place to leave.

LAURA   The unluckiest county in Ireland? Poor wee bastards.

FRANK   It's cold. Winter is coming. You have been punished in some way for knowing me. A good thing the sun awaits you.

LAURA   A good thing. Goodbye Frank. I'll write. *(exits. He watches her go)*

FRANK   You better.

> **FRANK** *sits down on a mound. He directs himself outwards and towards the earth.*

Years ago, when they brought you here to me, I made no fuss. I knew what would be done. I made a secret life for you here. I rode you through dark glades so that your long and graceful legs could still feel the joy of speed as land and air passed under you. I fed you and groomed you till I could see my own reflection in your skin. And time passed and we couldn't let you be discovered. So I gave you this home – all yours, private – in your prime. All these years you have lain undisturbed under a patchwork of leaves and sky and stars in this most fertile grave. You've taken your revenge. A child is dead from something you offered us for eating. An eye for an eye. Let me be now. Let me not hear that sound again, no matter how close it is. In return I will try to quiet myself, and make the distance from my anger long. And I'll wait. For signs of hope and your forgiveness.

Fade lights.

The End

STAGING NOTES:

Use same furniture for the two houses (Nancy's and Philip's). The large picture may be suspended, and reversed for Nancy's house.

The mushroom tunnels may be indicated by a row of dimly-lit light-bulbs/fluorescent lights. The containers may be on wheels. The lights go off when exiting the tunnels, and are dim when 'inside.' The wild mushrooms may be physical things or they may be 'imaginary'. The hut may either be imaginary or a wheeled-on contraption (stage-right), in which case the hut's light could employ one of the lightbulbs from the 'mushroom tunnel' row.

GLOSSARY OF TERMS

Shergar – was a racehorse supposedly kidnapped and murdered by the IRA in 1983. The exact whereabouts of his remains have never been located.

Padraig Pearse – was one of the leaders of the 1916 Easter Rising.

Tarry Flynn – is a prose work by Patrick Kavanagh.

Dues – contributions made by parishioners to the Catholic Church; envelopes sent out a number of times a year, often collected by voluntary church workers.

Property List

Fireplace – over the mantelpiece hangs a framed photograph of a young woman, with 'Raglan Road 1954' typed on the bottom (p1)

A bunch of wrapped blue carnations (p1)

Cereal (p1)

Vase (p1)

Newspaper (p1)

Radio (p1)

Two cups of tea (p4)

Bucket of fire fuel: briquettes, coal, stick, some rolled-up paper and some firelighters (p4)

Cigarette (p6)

TV (p6)

Post (p6)

Packet of envelopes (p6)

Fire stoke (p7)

Packing materials (p8)

Poly-tunnels covered in black plastic (p8)

Humidity and temperature apparatus (p8)

Lace gloves (p8)

Standard issue latex gloves (p8)

Thermometer (p10)

Punnets (p11)

Crate (p11)

Stack of crates (p11)

Cigarette (p14)

Cigarette (p16)

Radio (p19)

Compost (p25)

Over the mantelpiece hangs an enlarged colour photo of
    Nancy in a ballroom gown holding a trophy (p27)

Cigarette (p27)

Whiskey bottle in a cupboard underneath the television
    (p28)

Small table (p33)

Pots (p33)

Pans (p33)

Cutlery (p33)

Small stove (p33)

Two small wicker baskets (p33)

Two plates of cooked breakfast (p40)

Polishing his dancing shoes (p42)

Carnation on jacket lapel (p43)

Plates (p48)

Our Lady of Fatima Statue (p49)

Radio (p60)

Baskets (p60)

Long table (p66)

Barbecue (p64)

Ghetto blaster (p66)

Basket of wild mushrooms (p68)

Cassette (p70)

Tree stump (p72)

Cigarette (p72)

Radio (p79)

Compost (p84)

Costume:

Laura enters all dressed up (p42)

Lighting

Laura puts off the light (p2)

Philip puts on the light (p2)

Laura puts off the light (p2)

Philip puts on the light (p7)

Fade lights (p7)

Blackout (p18)

Fade Lights (p26)

Night-time (p27)

Fade lights (p32)

Bare bulb hangs from centre (p33)

Frank puts on the light (p38)

Fade lights (p41)

Blackout (p47)

Fade lights (p59)

Fade lights (p65)

Fade lights (p71)

Fade lights (p78)

Fade lights (p83)

Fade lights (p88)

Sound Effects

He puts on the radio (p2)

Philip puts on the TV by pressing the on/off switch. Now the TV and radio are on (p6)

Laura turns off the radio (p6)

Philip puts the TV off (p7)

The radio is on (p8)

The radio is on (p19)

Cacophony of snoring sounds (p27)

A scream is heard from Nancy's room (p27)

A scream is heard from Philip's room and there are loud thumping noises (p28)

The sound increases as the helicopter is overhead (p39)

Philip puts on his Frank Sinatra tape (p45)

Laura puts the music off (p45)

A knock on the door (p49)

Philip puts on some music – a scratched 78 of 'The Tennessee Waltz' (p52)

Loud bangs are heard (p52)

Laura rushes to stop the music (p52)

The sound dies away (p52)

There is a loud knock on the door (p53)

Sound of Philip's door opening (p59)

The radio is on (p60)

There is a ghetto blaster playing The Cult's 'She Sells Sanctuary' (p66)

Philip gestures to Owen to turn the music down – who does, just a little (p66)

Philip goes to the ghetto blaster and turns off the music (p67)

Music is put on (p70)

Tom – slamming the music off (p70)

Philip puts on his 'rebel songs' tape (p71)

Laura hears an approach (p72)

The radio is on (p79)

Owen changes the radio station (p79)

A helicopter can be heard in the distance. The sound is quite loud on stage and then fades away (p84)

Lightning Source UK Ltd.
Milton Keynes UK
UKOW06f1134260915

259288UK00001B/17/P